WISDOM OF WEALTHY ACHIEVERS

PHILIP BAKER

BY THE SAME AUTHOR

Secrets of Super Achievers
Attitudes of Amazing Achievers

Wisdom – The Forgotten Factor of Success

WISDOM OF WEALTHY ACHIEVERS

All Bible References are taken from the New International Version [Zondervan Bible Publishers, Grand Rapids, MI, 1984.] unless stated otherwise.

All enquiries regarding this publication and Phil Baker's speaking engagements, to be made to:

INSIDE-OUT Resources Inc.
PO Box 1339 . South Perth . Western Australia . 6951
T . [618] 9367 2190 F . [618] 9367 2190
E . webb@vianet.net.au

Printed by McPherson's Printing Group . Maryborough . Victoria . Australia

National Library of Australia . Canberra . Australia
ISBN: 0 9577020 2 7

"A CLEAR DISTINCTION MUST BE MADE BETWEEN OUR FINAL AIMS - THE ULTIMATE ACHIEVEMENTS THAT GIVE PURPOSE TO LIFE - AND THE MEANS THROUGH WHICH WE HOPE TO ATTAIN THEM. FOR EXAMPLE, MONEY IS NEVER A FINAL AIM; IT HAS NO VALUE IN ITSELF. IT CAN ONLY ACT AS A MEANS, HELPING US TO REACH SOME ULTIMATE GOAL WHICH, TO US, HAS INHERENT VALUE."

HANS SELYE

DEDICATED

TO THE

AUSSIE BATTLER

CONTENTS

INTRODUCTION

"ALL THAT GLISTENS..."

Last time I was in Los Angeles, I had breakfast with a friend. On this morning, however, the breakfast of hash browns, three eggs, toast, sausage links and coffee (all for $3.99) was rudely interrupted by a fight. A fracas had broken out at the back of the restaurant culminating with a man in his mid-thirties being dragged out of the place by the manager. As he passed our table, he was still shouting in colourful, cutting and non-ecclesiastical language about what he was going to do to his opponent if only he would come outside.

The protagonist wearing designer jeans and wrap-around sunglasses then just sat outside waiting. Within two minutes, I kid you not; four police cars had arrived (and I thought LA was a high crime zone). It all made for an interesting breakfast.

A little bit of investigation revealed that the fight had erupted because another customer was upset that our loud-mouthed friend was allowing his kids to run all through the restaurant and pour salt on people's meals. A punch in the face was his reward for pointing out his displeasure to their father. On leaving, we noticed our fighter's wife on her mobile, standing next to a new white convertible BMW. I remarked to my friend that it was amazing to me that someone who had built up a reasonable amount of wealth could be stupid enough to start hitting a total stranger at breakfast. My friend, a fellow author, wisely replied, "No, not wealthy - just high debt level."

Wealth, you see, is the fruit of wisdom. The discipline, planning and self-control necessary to establish financial independence, does not go losing its cool in moronic and rash ways. When the fool acquires wealth, it is predominantly due to luck or legacy. Given time, things will return to their proper level.

It is the contention of this book that, although wealth may come to some in fortuitous ways, this is the exception and not the rule. Wealth is not out of reach to us average folk on regular

"A MAN'S LIFE

DOES NOT

CONSIST IN THE

ABUNDANCE OF

HIS

POSSESSIONS."

JESUS (LUKE 12:15)

"WHEN ALL IS

SAID AND DONE

ABOUT FINANCIAL

ANALYSTS,

MORE IS SAID

THAN DONE."

wages who don't have a rich uncle or winning lottery ticket. It is not what we have but what we do with what we have that will make the difference over the long term. Wealth is not the fruit of income but of wisdom, and that wisdom is available to us all.

WISDOM, WEALTH AND THE ANCIENTS

In our study of wealthy achievers, we will discover that the present has no mortgage on truth. Indeed, much can be gleaned from the writings of ancient history, for the building of wealth is not a new thing. Well before Bill Gates, Wealthy Achievers were making their marks in the cities of northern Europe, the streets of Babylon and the markets of the Far East. The tools may have changed and wealth's measurement, management and manifestations may be different, but the underlying principles remain the same.

Unfortunately many of us have unknowingly become victims of what I call the "parochialism of the present". We have a tendency to look back in time with a patronising attitude towards the generations that came before us. After all, we have inter-planetary travel, personal computers and automatic flushing toilets. Yet, human progress over the last few thousand years is progress that has mainly had to do with superficial external rather than the substantial internal.

One could argue that the ancients had their act together a lot better than us in the things that really matter. Our superstitions are just as silly - our paranoia just as real. In fact our proneness to panic, in some areas, exceeds all previous generations. Robert Lacey & Danny Danziger point this out in their book, The Year 1000[1], when they observe that there was certainly very little of the hysteria regarding the approaching of their new millennium that we experienced moving into ours.

We might know more but we are not wiser. We have more information but less insight. Indeed maybe the two are connected. We pride ourselves on what we know… the increase of our knowledge, which we then think is thinking. Yet these brains of ours are more than just storage systems for mass data. They are meant to ponder and apply truth, not just to the career but to the character as well. The point must also be made that the population of this planet 5,000 years ago was not exactly made up of ignorant savages either. Studies in ancient cultures have revealed an amazing level of sophistication, not only in areas such as philosophy where Aristotle and Plato still rule supreme, but also in social organisation, education and the inculcation of values within each new generation.

Indeed, much of what we thought they were ignorant of has turned out to be myth. C S Lewis in the fifties and more recently Umberto Eco have made the point that the ancients were fully aware that the world was a sphere and a small object in a vast universe.

Ptolemy mentions this as far back as the fourth century BC, a truth that has been reiterated throughout the ages by writers such as Pythagoras, Plato, Euclid, Archimedes, Augustine, Dante, Origin, Ambrose, Aquinas and Roger Bacon. The controversy surrounding Columbus and his trips to the New World was not between the flat earthers and the rest, but rather one based on the size of the planet.

"The Sages of Salamanca had in fact made calculations more precise than his (Columbus) and they held that the earth, while assuredly round, was far more vast than the Genoese navigator believed, and therefore it was mad for him to attempt to circumnavigate it in order to reach the Orient by way of the Occident. Columbus, on the contrary, burning with a sacred fire, good navigator but bad astronomer, thought the earth smaller than it was. Naturally neither he nor the learned men of Salamanca suspected that between Europe and Asia there lay another continent."[2]

So, armed with a healthy respect for the previous and taking care that we do not fall into the ditch on the other side of this particular road - that of glorifying the past - let us study the subject at hand. It is highly beneficial, I have discovered, to look back in time at the wisdom of the ancients on wealth creation. It enables us to remove much of the clutter and techno-speak of our own time. Today, we are often confused and led astray by new-fangled investment opportunities or wealth-building strategies that are sophisticated yet stupid; impressive looking edifices built upon quicksand.

The foundations of wealth, however, have remained the same throughout human history. Many were penned by sages such as Solomon

“MONEY ISN’T EVERYTHING, BUT IT SURE KEEPS YOU IN TOUCH WITH YOUR CHILDREN.”

“We will loan you enough money to get you completely out of debt.”

Sign in a loan office.

who wrote his proverbs around 950 BC and since their time they have been respected for both their clarity and their hiddenness.

Indeed, in the first chapter of the Book of Proverbs, the point is made that wisdom is not always obvious. It has to be dug for, wrestled with and nutted out. Many such Proverbs are written in riddled form. It is not enough to read - one must study, think and apply.

WEALTH DEFINED - SO WHAT IS WEALTH ANYWAY?

When I was ten, wealthy meant owning the champion conker. The conker is the nut from the Chestnut tree through which we bored a hole, and then threaded a bit of string with a knot on the end. We would then take turns of hitting a friend's nut until one of them smashed. The winning nut was then a "oner", i.e. it had defeated one other nut. If your nut was a "fiver" and you beat someone else's that was a "tener", you automatically became a "fifteener". I think the champion nut when I was in boarding school was a "hundred-and-twentier" or some other similarly astronomical number. The kid who owned that nut was king.

When I was twelve, wealthy meant holding Sally's hand. It took me four weeks of mustering up the courage and a fight to beat her then-boyfriend before this wealth became mine, yet my treasure lasted only for another five days until she got off the liner we were on at her destined stop of Sydney. I continued on with my family to Auckland, New Zealand, where we were moving to from England.

In my teenage years, I came in contact with various other definitions of wealth: having a horse, living by the sea, owning your own Mk II Zephyr.[3]

Most people in their twenties and thirties think of wealth as simply an abundance of possessions or a high income - high being purely subjective, generally meaning anybody earning at least $20,000 more than you.

I once had a Bible College teacher who defined wealth as, "having more than enough" which may be why so many Christians for example, are philosophically against wealth. "We shouldn't have more than enough, we should have what we need. Anything else is wasteful, greedy or materialistic". Yet the Book of Proverbs and other ancient writings are pretty clear that wealth is not only a good thing, it is a desired thing, and for reasons far nobler than the ones its opponents proffer.

So, what is wealth? High consumption supported by high debt level? The company-leased Mercedes or the government-funded overseas junket? Is it flying first class on $300-$400,000 a year? Or is it, as Gordon Gecko would say, "being liquid... owning your own jet?"

It is important to have a clear understanding of what we are actually aiming for. If we define wealth in terms of car model, house size or earning capacity, we will head off on the journey wrong-footed and muddle-headed. We will discover that many of the luxury car driving, high income earning, and big house living individuals are not wealthy. They simply have large cash flow, and the cash flows in and the cash flows out and, while they are doing the hokey-pokey and turning around, the banks, leasing companies, travel agents and prestige car dealerships are getting wealthy.

When we use the word wealth, in this volume, I have in mind several different factors:

Number 1 - Wealth is About Process Rather Than Destination

Wealth is not seen in a magical set of figures but in how a life is organised, the direction one is moving, and the existence of a financial plan and percentages of funds invested and donated.

In other words, wealth not only looks at the breadth of the picture but considers the passing of time as well. It's a movie, not a photo. A snap shot of a high profile athlete, for example, would reveal high income levels. The movie would show that, on retirement from active competition, unless alternative plans are already being developed, earning capacity would diminish rapidly.

The movie, in other words, takes into account what will probably be happening in the years to come, both positive and negative.

That old joke... "How do you get a fool to have a million dollars by the time he is forty? Give him $10 million when he is 35..." rings true here.

Number 2 - Wealth Is About The Building Of Net Worth

Net worth is defined as the current value of one's assets less one's liabilities. In their book, The Millionaire Next Door, Thomas Stanley and William Danko point out that such a calculation should take into account both age and earning capacity.

For example, if your net worth is $350,000 and you are 35 years of age with an annual family income of $50,000, you are wealthier than the 65 year old on an income of $120,000 whose net worth is $700,000. The writers of this book actually include an equation, a rule of thumb, in computing where the line of wealth on this basis is. "Multiply your age by your realised pre-taxed annual household income from all sources except inheritances and divide by ten. This, less any inherited wealth, is what your net worth should be".[4]

They suggest that this figure should be doubled if one is serious about wealth creation. Such equations are merely opinion and other similar calculations could be made fixing the point of wealth higher or lower. What is important is that wealth is seen as a mixture of net worth, earning capacity and age.

Number 3 - Wealth Is How Long You Could Survive If You Lost Your Job

The point is not so much about what you have in the bank but about how much money is working for you. The majority of people work for money and when they stop working their income stops. If retrenchment takes place, within two weeks the bills are not getting paid. Such a hand-to-mouth existence is now considered culturally normal. That is, if our life is like this, we don't think anything of it.

"COMPOUND

INTEREST IS

THE EIGHTH

WONDER OF

THE WORLD."

"THE ECONOMY
DEPENDS AS
MUCH ON
ECONOMISTS AS
THE WEATHER
DOES ON THE
WEATHER
FORECASTERS."

Wealthy Achievers, on the other hand, are following a plan. A plan which puts aside money systematically and consistently and then employs it in earning more money. The amount being earned here is not really the issue. The question is, is this transition being made? Are we weaning ourselves off relying on our work onto relying on our money to work for us?

A family on an average income can make this transition depending upon their choice of investment in normally a 10 to 15 year period. There will suddenly come a moment in time when the money being earned by their money is equal to or more than the money being earned by them. At this point, if they so chose, they could stop working and keep living at the same level of lifestyle, theoretically forever.

When it comes to money sense, most of us are pretty dumb. We have to be hit in the face time and time again by stupid investments, speculative follies or ridiculous purchases and, even then, there if no telling if we will learn from these experiences the truth about money.

At one time, I had intended to call this volume Secrets of Wealth, not because its contents are filled with esoteric or mystical formulae, but because the pragmatic, common sense wisdom of wealth creation is known but not known or - if you like - known but not realised.

I often look through the tables of contents of various books thinking to myself, "I know that". But the truth is, I only really know it, if I am doing it. The theory matters little; the practice is what makes the difference. I challenge you, in fact, to ponder the previous definitions of wealth. If these describe you, then you probably don't need to read the book. Although, of course, if it does, you will be reading the book anyway, as you understand the importance of continued reinforcement of wealth creating truth.

I have also designed this book in such a way that it is not just about the theory of wealth but also encompasses the specifics. Not only what should I be doing, but also how should I be doing it? On the other hand, I have tried to resist the temptation of getting too detailed. There are many books on the market today that specialise in such minutiae. Due to changing tax laws and investment opportunities, they are constantly being produced and their information is vital once you get down to the actual brass tacks of phoning the broker, talking to the real estate agent or structuring your holdings in such a way as to minimise tax.

PART I

LAYING THE FOUNDATION

CHAPTER 1

THE WISDOM OF THE "WHY"

"Wealth is a Good Thing"

"IT'S JUST AS EASY TO LIVE WELL WHEN YOU'RE POOR, AS WHEN YOU'RE RICH - BUT WHEN YOU'RE POOR, IT'S MUCH CHEAPER."

The first step on our journey of wealth creation is to realise that the journey, in itself, is a good journey. Good in the sense of moral or right. Many never set out because deep down they have bought into the thinking that says the accumulation of wealth is questionable, superficial or suspect.

There is an unspoken value that permeates many Christian churches, for example, that suggests deeper poverty equates to deeper spirituality. That God is on the side of the poor (which He is) and is against the rich (which He isn't). Therefore, it is a lot easier not to build wealth because, by so doing, you open yourself to all sorts of innuendo, jealousies and divine disfavour. Play it safe, don't rise above the norm, live up to (read "down to") the expectations of family and friends.

With this kind of belief system, all talk about financial independence is just that - talk. The road to wealth, however, is mostly uphill. Only the determined and convinced will make it. Lingering doubts or an unquiet conscience will continually erode our capacity to make the trip. So let us confront head on some of the mindsets and myths that argue against wealth creation and by so doing discover what the Wealthy Achievers' philosophical foundation actually is.

Myth 1 - Wealth Leads to Pride and Materialism

Whilst it is true that the ranks of the well-to-do contain the avaricious and the arrogant, it is demonstrably not because the accumulation of wealth is linked to such characteristics. Pride and materialism are not simply the result of having more. They are evidenced in the lives of those who have nothing as well as those who have much. Greed is not only found in Wall Street boardrooms but also on suburban streets and third world shanty-towns.

In my observation, it seems that an individual with a tendency towards self-absorption will find increased cash flow fuelling their weakness. On the other hand, if they were to lose everything, this too would push them further into the abyss of selfishness and hardened pride. Money may magnify our strengths and our weaknesses but it certainly doesn't create them. Even if one could establish a causal link between money and materialism, such a link would not be universal. We all know people for whom this would not be true.

The most that could be said is that sometimes money could lead to pride and materialism.

Yet this in itself does not make the journey to wealth invalid or detrimental. It is a little like saying that marriage can lead to divorce, work may lead to injury or even life will lead to death. Whilst these are all true, they are not valid arguments against marriage, work or life. I am aware of the statistics on relationships but I still believe marriage is wonderful and will do everything in my power to stay married and happy. I am also aware of the dangers and opportunities that can come into play when our financial world begins to grow. But I will still pursue the increase of net worth, because it is a good thing, a right thing and if used and handled with care will add value, not only to my life but to many others as well.

The Wealthy Achiever realises that just because some allow an increase in net worth to be a catalyst for increased personality dysfunction, this is no reason to withdraw. On the contrary - to do so would vacate the field to the crass and ignoble at a time when better role models are called for.

Myth 2 - The Accumulation of Wealth Funds Inequality

The ideal of socialism is one that captures the heart and attempts to take the high moral ground. Pragmatically, however, it just doesn't work. Is it right that the lazy and the diligent get the same reward? That the one who saves and sows has the same harvest as the one who does not? Is it right to remove the consequences from caution-free living, so that the gullible and rash live life penalty free? Should the gambler or the sex addict not feel the pain or experience the cost of squandering their pay packets at Black Jack or the brothel? Surely, any attempt to level the field, as it were, is self-defeating and wrong-headed. If everyone gets the same regardless of what they do, then let us do exactly what we want. Consequence is removed from action, repercussions from decisions. I for one would certainly not want to live in such a world.

Much of the inequality in society is immoral and unfair, but if I use this as an excuse not to move towards wealth, I too have become part of the problem. Wealthy Achievers realise that the answer is for good people, generous people,

people with high ideals and fine character to work at obtaining wealth so that they can do something that will ease the pain of our community. Why allow the province of prosperity to become the sole domain of the greedy and the uncaring?

Indeed the great charity and non-profit organisations that work the hardest in our society to alleviate suffering and input answers to the culture's most pressing needs, are funded by and large by the Wealthy Achiever.

Obviously for some, this may be a gesture that eases conscience but for many it is their mandate... their joy and their destiny.

Myth 3 - The More I Get, The Less There Is For Someone Else

This is a variation to the second objection, and is based on a faulty idea of economics. Wealth is not limited. There is not only so much to go around. Our financial world is not a pie with limited slices. Wealth is created, created by people who apply their ideas and diligence to

"OF ALL THE
ADVANTAGES
WHICH CAME TO
ME AS A YOUNG
MAN, I BELIEVE IT
TO BE
DEMONSTRABLY
TRUE THAT
POVERTY IS THE
GREATEST."

JOSEPH HOLLAND

"Empty pockets never held anyone back. It's only empty heads and empty hearts that do it."

Norman Vincent Peale

their world. The more I work, invest and give, the more there is.

I wrote of this in greater detail in my first book, Secrets of Super Achievers.

Super Achievers understand that individual success does not necessarily mean the failure of others. They have, what I term as, an abundance mentality. They want to succeed, they want to do well, and they want to reach their goals. And they are not in any way hampered by a feeling of guilt. Guilt only accompanies those who think in terms of, "I win, you lose".

The scarcity mentality sees the economic world as a kind of pie with only so many pieces to go around. The more I get on my plate, the less for everyone else. If I consider this a good thing, I become confrontational and competitive. If I consider this a bad thing, I become demotivated and guilty of success. In an effort to appease conscience, I lower my standards and give in to the falseness of the "tall poppy syndrome". I settle for mediocrity.

The truth is, life is not like a pie. The more I receive does not mean the less everyone else receives. Conrad Black the Canadian media baron puts it this way, "It is the myth of the left and one of the wellsprings of the pervasive spirit of envy that the success of a person implies the failure or exploitation of someone else. Our economic system is not based upon single combat war or a zero-sum game."

Life is more like a river. There is plenty for everyone. The pie analogy only works, thinking of it in purely economic terms, if we give to the pie the possibility of expansion. Creativity, entrepreneurship and individual effort cause such growth.

Wealth then is not limited to physical resource but to human creativity. The nation of Singapore is a good example of this. Over the last 40 years and without the necessary raw materials, physical space or rich arable farmland, this country has grown its economy considerably. They simply added to the picture, initiative, dreams, entrepreneurship, wisdom and persistence.[5]

Myth 4 - God... Friends... Government Will Provide

Having been a Christian for some 25 years, I have heard my fair share of, "God will provide" messages. Not that there is anything wrong with that, as Jerry Seinfeld would say. What upsets me is that such teaching rarely gets into the specifics of how God supplies.

Ostensibly, what is presented tends to be a simplistic patter regarding the importance of giving and faith, and somehow, in some way, something good will happen to you. How much everyone should give is explained with great specificity. But after that, things get nebulous and esoteric. The problem is not in what is being said but in what is not being said. Giving is one of the building blocks employed by the Wealthy Achiever, but it is only one. Without the others, not much will happen except for the fact that many honest, God-fearing people will become disillusioned.

The most dangerous aspect of this teaching is that it actually works against wisdom in that giving and faith are presented as the only keys. To have a financial plan and then work towards savings, investment and asset acquisition is seen not only as unnecessary but also as an invalidation of trust in a supreme benefactor.

Unfortunately, many who languish in the financial doldrums do so because of failure to take ownership for their own money management and prosperity.

If family, friends or religious faith are seen as our rescuer, then we will continuously put ourselves in situations from which we need rescuing.

Wealthy Achievers use God-given privileges but don't expect God, or anybody else, to do what they themselves realise lies within their own sphere of responsibility.

Myth 5 - The Journey Towards Wealth Is Intrinsically Selfish

Undoubtedly, many try to get rich for riches' sake. Their motive is selfishness. Their god is money. The more the merrier.

"PROBLEMS

ARE ONLY

OPPORTUNITIES

IN WORK

CLOTHES."

HENRY KAISER

"I HAVE TRIED TO
TEACH PEOPLE THAT
THERE ARE THREE
KICKS IN EVERY
DOLLAR: ONE, WHEN
YOU MAKE IT - AND
HOW I LOVE TO MAKE
A DOLLAR; TWO,
WHEN YOU HAVE IT -
AND I HAVE THE
YANKEE LUST FOR
SAVING. THE THIRD
KICK IS WHEN YOU
GIVE IT AWAY - AND
IT IS THE BIGGEST
KICK OF ALL."

WILLIAM ALLEN WHITE

The ancient Book of Proverbs promotes wealth as a side benefit of wisdom. Wisdom essentially is outward focussed; that is, the goal of wealth is pursued for what one can give, what one can do to make, not only one's life, but also one's world, a better place. As God said to Abraham, "I will bless you and you can be a blessing".[6]

The purpose of prosperity is not self-indulgence but difference-making. The idea is to become a channel not a vessel. One can build a large house to be a dwelling for many or one can build it as an icon to self. The former produces meaning and makes sense of wealth creation. The latter is vulgar and banal. The means must not become the end.

My vision for life - for what I feel I am meant to do - requires money, but money is not part of the vision. Those who want a million dollars, but don't know what they would do with it, have allowed money to dominate. The props are not meant to be the action, the frame the picture, or the stadium the game. Wealth has far loftier reasons than selfishness and pure indulgence.

MYTH 6 - I DON'T DESERVE IT

Somehow in our minds, many of us have the idea that some people should have money, and some probably should not. This seems strange in a world where egalitarianism has triumphed over the class system but old ways of thinking die hard. Why don't you deserve it? Whatever reason we give, wealthy people around the world echo our thoughts and share our experiences, yet they do not allow such thinking to become their dominant reality. You may have come from a poor family, a broken home, the country, or the inner city. You may be too small, too tall, too clever or too stupid. You could be timid or talkative, polished or primitive. You might even have weaknesses (who doesn't?) or flaws (form a line!). What we must understand is that wealth is not handed out to the perfect or the good looking but to all who would set their sails to catch the prevailing wind of truth. You don't have to be brilliant, just prepared to do the right thing over the long haul.

I like the story of one school reunion. Everyone was amazed when the dumbest kid in the class arrived in a limousine. He had, since leaving school, built up a very successful company and had become on the way a multimillionaire. During the evening, someone summoned up the courage to ask how he had achieved this. "All I do", he replied, "is buy these little toys for $2 and then sell them for $5. It is amazing how much money you can make with only a 3% mark-up!"

In the final analysis, action counts more than ability and movement more than mathematics, in the journey towards wealth.

Wealthy Achievers throughout history would bid us realise that it is okay to be wealthy. In fact, wealth is one of the side products of wise living. Once wealth is acquired, wisdom will help us use it generously and prudently. However, we must give ourselves permission to be wealthy for if we cannot, then the foundation of our financial wellbeing will be inadequate to build upon and consequently our journey forward will be fatally frustrated. On the other hand, if our thinking is right, our motives pure and our conscience clear, then the building of wealth becomes a joyful and destiny-achieving endeavour.

CHAPTER 2

THE WISDOM OF THE 'WHEN'

"The Slow Build"

"BY WISDOM A HOUSE IS BUILT AND THROUGH UNDERSTANDING IT IS ESTABLISHED. THROUGH KNOWLEDGE ITS ROOMS ARE FILLED WITH RARE AND BEAUTIFUL TREASURES."[7]

The metaphor of building a house is an apt one when considering wealth creation. It takes time, effort and patience. Things hardly ever go as smoothly as they were planned.

Architects must be employed, foundations laid and then slowly the structure begins to rise - brick or plank at a time. It is a process not an event.

Unfortunately, many people's approach to financial increase is to look for the big events - the opportunities of a lifetime, pots of gold under rainbows and get-rich-with-speed schemes. The slow step-by-step movement towards our goal is perceived to be to boring, too habit-based, too future-orientated. The Wealthy Achiever has to, in this regard, swim against the current. We live in a consume-it-now culture. We don't want to wait; we want convenience, speed and instant gratification. Yet such an approach is wrong-headed and corrosive to genuine wealth creation.

I recently watched an advertisement on TV promising no deposit, no repayments for six months and no interest payable for that six-month period. While these wonderful, life-enriching statements are being made, small print is speeding along the bottom of the screen. I had to watch several times to read it all: "Once repayments begin interest charged will be at 25%."

There is no doubt building a house on sand is fast. Yet the price must still be paid, usually when such a house gets flattened as the first storm makes its presence felt.

The allure of the instant is powerful, the numbers bounce around on the lottery machine and if ours come out, life is changed in a moment. Every time one walks through a casino or a club, one sees this attraction at work. Hundreds of pleasure seeking yet passionless people mindlessly feeding coins into bright and beautiful jackpot-promising machines.

It is not uncommon to see on our beaches the hopeful fossicker armed with a metal detector, in search of rich discoveries - the Rolex lost in the sand, the gold bullion from the Spanish wreck. The thrill of the chase and the promise of a sudden change in fortune will result in hundreds of hours being lost and an incredible amount of money spent in finding that lost dollar coin. Yet wisdom is not so arbitrary. It doesn't bring wealth to our lives like a genie in a bottle. It simply points us in the right direction and bids us take a step, and then another, and then another, and then another.

If I save a dollar a day, and then employ the effects of compound interest, it will grow to well over $200,000 at the end of a working life. $5 a day will turn into over a million dollars. We may start off small, but small grows.[8] The principle of sowing and reaping, of multiplication, is all about this. Multiplication already implies we have what we need. It is not out there somewhere, waiting to be discovered. It is already present within. What we must do is use it, plant it and nurture it. We have time, we have process and we have seed. Therefore, we have everything we need. The longer we put off beginning, the harder it will be. The tyranny of the sudden must be destroyed.

We find it easy to overlook the small. Large amounts grab our attention whilst widow's mites are ignored. Yet, wealth is built on little amounts over time. Small change adds up.

Let's say you are twenty and you have a 20-year-old friend who likes coffee as much as you. Let's say also that, on average, you drink three cappuccinos a day at a cost of $2.20 each. Suddenly your mate announces he is giving up the caffeine and instead will invest the $200 a month he is now spending in a solid share

"BUDGET: A
MATHEMATICAL
CONFIRMATION
OF YOUR
SUSPICIONS."

A A LATIMER

"Investors operate with limited funds and limited intelligence. They do not need to know everything. As long as they understand something better than others, they have an edge."

George Soros

or property trust. As coffee rises with inflation, so he increases his monthly payments to match your cappuccino costs. At age 65, if the return on his net investment is 9% and if inflation averages 4%, the difference between you and your friend is amazing. While you have stained teeth and somewhat of a wide-eyed look, your mate will have nearly $2.5 million - all the result of giving up a few cups of coffee.

(Let me hasten to add that the taste of great espresso over a lifetime would be considered by many (the author included) to be invaluable. The example is given purely to illustrate the mathematics, and should not in any way be seen as a recommended course of action!)

"Well", I can hear you saying. "It's all very well to talk about building, but how do I start? What materials do I use? What plan should I follow?" Such considerations are important and indeed Part 2 of this book will look at the specifics that the Wealthy Achiever employs. What is essential here is that we are prepared for the slow build. We are not looking for hare-brained schemes that double our money in a month. For some of us this kind of thinking is very difficult, we almost need to have a personal paradigm shift. For every disciplined step-by-step person, there seem to be ten who are sporadic, spontaneous and feel that a life that slowly builds wealth would be a life given over to parsimonious and fun-killing boredom.

There are two ways to build. One is to build only with the finished product in mind and the days are endured as the project slowly takes shape. The other is to become a builder. That is to actually enjoy the process itself. The fun is not only discovered when the destination is reached but is enjoyed every step of the journey. So it is with wealth creation. We must celebrate the process and reward ourselves when small goals are achieved along the way.

True freedom and joy are experienced by those who have their spending in check and their debts under control. The new car bought with the hefty loan or the clothes with the credit card at its max erode the very pleasure of the goods themselves. The truth is, of course, that those who are involved in the process of building wealth actually have better fun, less angst and more to smile about than the big spenders, who tend to smile a lot on the outside but turn in their beds at night. The book, The Millionaire Next Door by Thomas Stanley and William Danko[9], examines the life of two high-income surgeons. Both were earning over $700,000 a year, yet how they handled their money differed significantly. One was a builder of wealth, the other a spender of it. In comparing their concerns, fears and worries, it was discovered that the spender had a much higher level of anxiety in many different areas than that of the builder - this despite being on such a high salary. Their comparative net worth reveals much.

Remember that here we have two people on the same income within the same profession. The spender had a net worth of $400,000, the builder $7.5 million. My point is, while the house is being built, life can be fun and, once it is built, life gets really exciting. However, the spender is always aware something is not quite right and, as life speeds by, the price he or she pays for this lack of foresight becomes more and more telling.

CHAPTER 3

THE WISDOM OF THE 'HOW'

"ALL JUNIOR EXECUTIVES SHOULD KNOW THAT IF THEY WORK HARD, TEN HOURS A DAY EVERY DAY, THEY COULD BE PROMOTED TO SENIOR EXECUTIVES SO THEY CAN WORK HARD FOR 14 HOURS A DAY."

JOHN CAPOZZI

There is a sequence to building. One can hardly start off with the roof before the walls are up, or begin the walls before the foundation has been laid. So it is with building wealth. We have started off with the general and we are now moving to the specific. If you like, each of these principles is like a serving bowl. The first one, "The Why of Wealth" is the largest of all. Within that sits the second, "The When"; and now the final foundational principle - "The How". Indeed, the specifics that follow in Part 2 are smaller bowls again, with each one fitting in sequence within the one before. Or to use a different metaphor, a series of steps that in most cases have to be completed or at least understood and accepted before the next one is really do-able.

In order to build wealth one must have a plan. There must be a map upon which we can chart our progress. In the same way there are many different ways to get from, say, Auckland, New Zealand to London, England. One can go via Sydney and Singapore, or Perth and Johannesburg or - by virtue of our planet being round - one could head off in the opposite direction to Los Angeles and then on to London. Either way, although the specifics may differ, there are some underlying principles that remain the same. One must leave, one must travel towards the destination, one must keep moving etc. etc.

"A COMPANY WITH NO DEBT ON ITS BALANCE SHEET WILL FIND IT VERY DIFFICULT TO GO BANKRUPT."

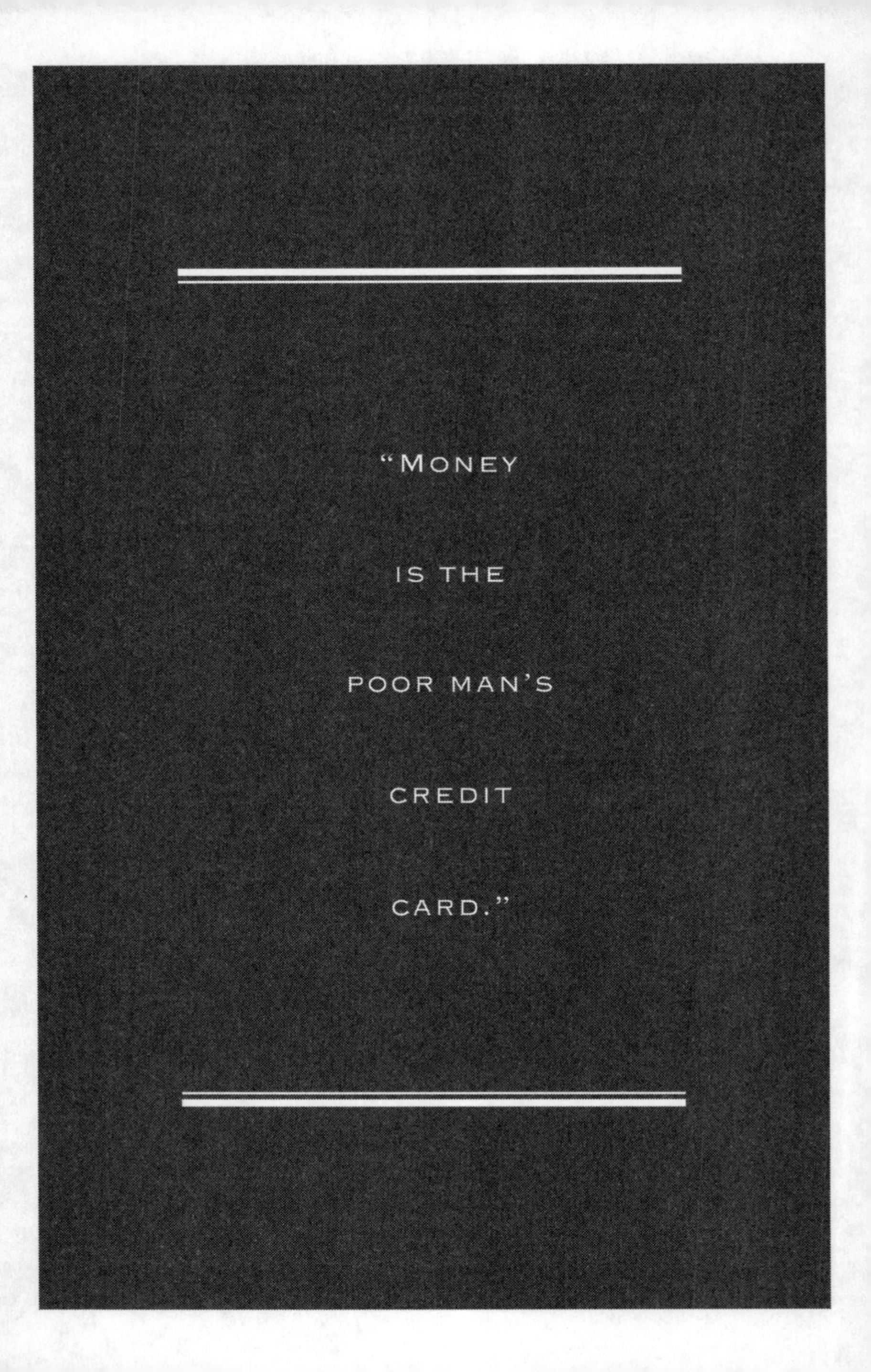
"Money
is the
poor man's
credit
card."

In the same way there are countless financial plans available on the market today, as well as countless individual ways people go about ensuring financial security. The common denominator is the existence of a plan. The best plans also include a way of measuring progress - short-term inbuilt goals that not only provide direction, but supply the energy and fuel for motivation as well.

One does not meander towards wealth or drift into its arms on the whims of the current. The current is contrary, the drifters head for the rocks. Wealth, like a house, has to be intended; it doesn't just happen. This wisdom, of course, is true for every area of life. Great lives, great marriages, great churches, great businesses are all the results of designs and strategies acted upon.

To put it another way, the road to wealth is uphill all the way. It takes energy and forethought to proceed. I wish life wasn't this way. It would be wonderful if the garden grew flowers and vegetables without cultivation. Unfortunately, however, when left by itself, only weeds prosper and grow. The vehicle left alone in the garage will begin to wind down as rust and corrosion slowly dominate.

Scientists call this the law of entropy or the third law of thermo-dynamics. That is, in any closed system, all things being equal, order will flow to disorder; organisation to chaos; the complex to simple; my tidy desk to the dishevelled pile of papers it is now!

The following then is a list of some of the basic components that the Wealthy Achiever utilises in the building of net worth.

Number 1 - The Plan

The first stage, of course, is to find the type of plan that fits your circumstances the best. I am not only talking here about the obvious, such as family, age and income, but also such things as personal idiosyncrasies, passions and personal knowledge base. There is no point choosing stamps as an investment vehicle, for example, if you don't actually have an interest in them. However, if it has always been a hobby and you are somewhat of an expert then maybe for you this would prove to be an excellent vehicle. Yet beware the dangers of loving too much. The wine connoisseur who chooses to invest in wine should not do so just because he likes to drink the stuff. The constant sampling of the cellar "just to make sure it is in prime condition" will erode profit with great speed (though I must add a most enjoyable way of doing so!). No, the wine lover may choose wine only because he understands the market, has legitimate sources of supply and a guaranteed way of selling when the time comes.

Number 2 - Eradicate Debt

Any plan worth its salt will quickly lower spending below income and apply the margin to debt reduction. The chapter on debt in the next section will look at this step in greater detail, but it is sufficient to say here that the presence of large short-term debt will do more than anything else to dampen life and block the road towards financial security. As somebody once observed, "when you are nostril deep in debt, any ripple is life-threatening."

Number 3 - Promote Frugality

The great pleasures in life are rarely expensive: wrestling with the two-year-old on the floor; walking along the beach; a summer barbeque with friends; making love to your spouse. Yet no one is paying for this truth to be advertised. What we tend to be exposed to all the time is the latest model Jaguar, the designer suits, the $800 watch. I have no problem with people buying such things provided they are buying them as a fruit of their wealth, not as a means to reaching it. As one recent study discovered, most of the purchasers of luxury goods are not Wealthy Achievers, rather they are high-income individuals who have bought into the lie of image at the expense of their own financial security.

Number 4 - Saving and Investing

The reason for frugality and the eradication of debt is, of course, to create savings for investment. There is not a lot to be gained in saving for saving's sake. At the point of writing, money left in the bank earning the regular interest rate will probably not even out-pace inflation. Money needs to be saved so that it can be invested, and investments must be chosen that not only appreciate but also produce income back into the savings and investment coffers.

There are hundreds of investment opportunities; some good, some mediocre and some downright terrible. Later on we will look at this area in more detail and, I hope, increase our investment IQ so that we will be able to navigate our way safely through these waters.

Number 5 - Plan to Give

The best plans I have encountered have a giving component written into them. That is, giving is not seen as a result once wealth has been acquired, but as a necessary part of the process. The fact is that miserly people throughout history have always been the most miserable. They may have financial wealth but they certainly are not wealthy in the areas of relationships, meaning or fulfilment. Generosity, on the other hand, seems to be tied to such things. In fact, if you think of the most generous people you know, and the stingiest people you know, invariably the former will also be the happiest and the latter the most depressed.

One such very general plan is called the "10:10:80 Plan" which basically says that the first 10% of your income should be given away to people in need, the local church, the non-profit organisation, to the people who are actually making a difference in our community.

The second 10% should be what you pay yourself. There is no point in working hard all week long in order to pay everybody else. The one who does the work should receive something for it. This 10% then is put aside for savings and investment.

What I like about this plan is that generosity is very much a factored part of it. You might, of course, be thinking to yourself as you read these words, "There is no way I could live off 80% of my income. It's all I can do right now to survive on the 100%." Whilst this may be true in a few situations, for the majority of us, if we suddenly received a reduction in our salary by 20% we would still go on living. We would have to change our spending habits, of course, our lifestyle, cut off a few credit cards,

"ANY FOOL

CAN MAKE

MONEY

- A WEALTHY

PERSON

KNOWS

HOW TO

SPEND IT."

"HERE IS
A USEFUL
SHOPPING TIP...
YOU CAN GET A
PAIR OF SHOES
FOR $2.00 AT
BOWLING
ALLEYS."

even move house. But survive we would. Life would go on. The "10:10:80 Plan" suggests that we should do it for ourselves rather than having it enforced on us by 'the slings and arrows of outrageous fortune'.

If you run the figures on this plan, it is interesting to see the results. Let's say you are 25 years old and earning $25,000 a year. You decide to apply this plan to your life for a 20-year period. Let us assume that your income does not go up at all during that period of time, and that you simply put the money in a bank earning a compound interest rate of 10%. At the end of a 20-year run, you would have given over $50,000 away, and would have $85,000 sitting in the bank.

To give another example, let's say you are 35 years of age and earning $40,000. On the same 20-year run, you would have given $80,000 away and saved over $170,000. Or to take one final example, the 45-year-old earning $80,000 a year, following the 10:10:80 Plan for a 20-year period would give $160,000 away and at the same time save nearly $350,000. If these monies were invested in appreciating and income-producing assets, the figures would be a lot higher.

The reason I feel that generosity must be part of the journey and not simply one of the results of any plan is that generosity, like savings and discipline, is a habit. If one never gives along the way, it will almost be impossible to start giving when you arrive. I also believe it is a lot harder to reach the destination if giving is not part and parcel of who you have become.

WORK THE PLAN

"He who works his land will have abundant food, but he who chases fantasies lacks judgement."[10]

Once a plan has been researched and formulated, it must be enacted. It must move from the notebook to life, from theory to reality, from a good idea to day-to-day lifestyle. Yet this is the most difficult thing of all. It is easy to buy a book like the one you now hold in your hand, to read it and then to commend oneself with words like, "I know all about financial management - I've just read the book."

Wisdom, however, is seen not in knowledge, but in action. Indeed, the difference between wisdom and knowledge is what we do about it. I knew about the importance of savings over 18 years ago. I remember going to a seminar where the speaker spoke about financial independence not being a function of income but a function of planning. That too many people choose the ice cream today rather than the bicycle tomorrow. They sabotage their future to fulfil the whims of the present. I sat there, writing notes furiously and commending myself that I was smart enough to be at the seminar, to write down such jewels of wisdom. Yet a decade later, I still had not enacted the very principles I had written down. This is why the realm of the wise is not prejudiced towards the intellectual. It is not a matter of how much we understand but a matter of how much we do. A certain level of knowledge, of course, is necessary but so many times knowledge puffs up, it substitutes for action and deludes us into thinking that we are ahead of the game.

The key is having a plan and following it over time. As I write these words, I could only think what my life would be like now if I had begun my plan some 15 years earlier. And if I hadn't bothered to have one now, in 15 years time I would still be rueing the fact.

So the high-powered lawyer or surgeon spends away on image, while the poorly educated immigrant lives life frugally and goes about buying property whenever he is able. Give this process ten to twenty years and the wisdom of action is clearly seen, as the now middle-aged debt-laden lawyer finds himself working almost exclusively for the wealthy land-owning immigrant. And even though he pulls up in his Porsche, alongside the beat-up pick-up truck of his new employer, he still doesn't get it. Sometimes smart people can be so stupid.

"NEVER PICK

A STOCK

- PICK GOOD

MANAGEMENT."

PART II

BUILDING THE HOUSE

CHAPTER 4

FLIRTING WITH FRUGALITY

"IN THE HOUSE OF THE WISE ARE STORES OF CHOICE FOOD AND OIL. BUT A FOOLISH MAN DEVOURS ALL HE HAS."[11]

In the 80's it was all about spending more than you actually had. Marks were given for the degree of difficulty required in juggling the various sources of short-term debt that made such a lifestyle possible. However, in the new millennium the word frugality is slowly but surely gaining a following.

[Maybe it was the way I was brought up, but I can clearly remember believing that the goal of financial planning was to time cash flow in such a way that all money was gone when the next week's pay arrived. The name of the game was to use it all and points were deducted for outstanding positive balances.]

Now some people find this particular secret easy to master. One couple I know actually enjoyed .... enjoyed eating polony sandwiches every day for lunch, and when I say "every day", I mean "every day... for years!". Simple living for them was not a financial necessity. It was choice and they preferred it that way... I think I hate them. My problem is that when I go into a store to pick a shirt or a tie, the one I like is invariably the most expensive one. I would love, one day, to pick the cheapest one, not because it was the cheapest but because I liked it and then found out it was the cheapest. I like nice food, good hotels, leather upholstery; yet, unless I embrace the concept of frugality, I will spend myself into oblivion.

So slowly I have been learning. I now know where the cheap or free parking is in the city and park there, choosing to walk a little further, which is both more enjoyable and healthier. When I have breakfast meetings, I always pick the same café - good coffee plus one egg on toast for less than $5.00 (which for Australia is very good and America very expensive). I only buy clothes on sale and only what I need. Gradually the new frugal me is taking over from the old buy-it-now, think-about-it-later, Phil Baker.

DON'T BE CHEAP..... BE FRUGAL

Before my spender friends hurl abuse at me and call me cheap, let me point out the difference between being frugal and cheap. Andrew Tobias does this well in his book, My Vast Fortune.[12] He illustrates frugality as not using the mini bar in the hotel room or if you do, restocking it from the grocery store on the corner. Frugal is turning the lights out when you are leaving the room. Frugal is buying home-brand sugar. Cheap, on the other hand, is buying home-brand coffee! It is selecting mediocrity over quality or buying the greatly reduced cashmere jumper with red ink on it as George Kastanza did on Seinfeld to impress a friend with his generosity. Cheap normally involves short-changing other people.

Let me reiterate. The reason frugality is so important is because financial independence is not about what you earn as much as it is about what you are able to keep. It is not just offence but defence that wins the game.

In one study of millionaires in America,[13] it was discovered that the lesson of frugality was the key difference that separated the wealthy from the high earner. Defence made the difference.

50% of the millionaires studied had never spent more than $235 on a watch, $399 on a suit or $140 on a pair of shoes.

For every millionaire owner of a suit over $1,000 there were six owners in the $50,000-$200,000 salary range.

One in four millionaires had never spent more than $100 on a pair of shoes and only 1 in 10 had exceeded the $300 mark. Yet for every one millionaire purchaser of shoes in that range there were eight non-millionaires.

These figures I found astounding… I sort of just imagined that millionaires - people who had built wealth - were the big spenders. It

"I BELIEVE

WE SHOULD ALL

PAY OUR TAX

BILL WITH A

SMILE. I TRIED...

BUT THEY

WANTED CASH!"

"You can't

have

everything.

Where would

you put

it?"

Stephen Wright

amazed me, for example, to find that 1 in 10 had never spent more than $47 on a watch.

I have come to believe that most of the spending on luxury goods is nothing more than monetary masturbation. I am sorry to put it so crudely, but why would anyone spend $3,000 on a watch other than to make a statement that is essentially all about self-absorption.

The high debt-level big spender lacks the secrets of the Wealthy Achiever. He or she thinks that spending up big is a sign of personal superiority. Yet the majority of such acquisition is simply an attempt to wallpaper over cracks in the soul.

Buying self-worth in such a way will always prove to be too expensive.

THE HIDDEN MOTIVES OF SPENDING

We do not always spend rationally... indeed there are often hidden agendas of which we ourselves may be unaware. The first key in controlling our spending habits is to find out why we buy as we do. Do we need that extra clarity in the sound system, grunt in the engine, or name on our golf clubs for ourselves? Or are there more sinister reasons lurking in our psyche? Bill Hybels, pastor of Willow Creek Church in Chicago, in a recent message listed the different types of spenders he had observed.[14]

Number 1 - Impulsive Spender

This is spending without forethought; no intention, just plain unadulterated spontaneity. Walking innocently through the department store when a red light flashes and an unwanted item just becomes 50% cheaper. So the bargain is grabbed on a wave of urgency and emotion. What the spender of this ilk must realise is that things will always be on sale. Persian rugs are always half price.

The impulse buyers end up with lots of things they don't want and have probably spent more for them than they needed to. Plan purchasing, shop around and then buy out of a knowledge base. Spontaneous spending rarely has the luxury of comparison.

Number 2 - Compulsive Spender

This is when our spending is not because we need the something we are buying but that we need to buy something. We purchase as a means to escape a hurt or medicate an internal pain. I am depressed… I'm going shopping. This temporary high anaesthetises, but such a medicine proves an expensive and ineffective cure, especially if the reason for the depression was high debt level. The answer is to get help, not from the shopping guide, but from the trained counsellor, friend or local church, or simply to find another outlet for our pain. Volunteering within some service organisation, going for a walk or a run or simply spending a leisurely hour in a museum will not only be kinder on our wallet but will add value to our life as well.

Number 3 - Revenge Spender

Okay, so I've been on a budget all year. I've been good, I've saved, but now I'm going to have a break… after all, I deserve it. I need a week of fun and take revenge on this stupid budget! So, within a few days, several months of good habits are obliterated.

If you feel this way, then hit a wall or have a cold shower. If you must splurge, then plan it into your budget. The short term spending frenzy only feels good for the short term whilst years of financial freedom are sacrificed at its insistence. Remember, the time will come when such a splurge will not be fatal.

Number 4 - Boredom Spender

Shopping has moved from chore to recreation, from necessity to hobby. The mall is where you go when you have nothing else to do. We wander, we saunter and invariably it is a costly walk. If shopping is what you do when you get bored, don't allow yourself to get bored! Walk by the river, visit a friend, volunteer at a church, visit a hospital or prison but don't spend any more money. Go read a book… from the library, unless it happens to be this book, which I think needs to be invested in personally so as to receive its full benefit!

Number 5 - Status Spender

We worry so much about what other people think. When we buy primarily in consideration of others with a desire to impress them, we have begun to slide down an ever-steepening slope.

A friend of mine had a game of golf at a charity do a while back. He happened to be grouped with three business tycoons, each of whom owned a jet. The conversation inevitably turned to aviation when one of them announced he has just ordered the new Falcon with all the added extras. The eyes of the others grew large with envy. My friend noticed that their two-year-old jets were no longer good enough; they too must now move up a rung.

If you care what other people think, when are you going to stop? The sooner we realise we are not what we own, the better. Harping back to the study of millionaires, the majority of them had broken out of the buy-for-status cycle.

Only 23.5% of them, for example, had new cars. Most had not spent more than $25,000 on a vehicle and 30% had spent $19,500 or less.

NUMBER 6 - SPECIAL INTEREST SPENDER

Most of us have an Achilles heel, something that we find very hard to pass by. If not controlled, such a frailty can prove fatal.

My own weakness is books. Books, books and more books - especially old ones. When I visit a new town it is not long before I have visited all the bookshops. Now, I do look for bargains, but if I find something I want which I haven't got, I can quickly and convincingly win the argument against my conscience. My library, as a result, is extensive. But many of the volumes will spend the rest of my life lining the shelves, never to be taken down again.

I have found some beauties over the years and, of course, I never call it spending... I'm investing. Yet, if the truth be known, I will never sell them and they will never earn any money. But they are so... nice. They include:

- A 1575 copy of Eusebius Church History;

"YOU FEED

YOUR EGO

OR

YOU FEED

YOUR FAMILY."

JIM ROHN

"All great masters are distinguished by the power of adding a second, a third and perhaps a fourth step in a continuous line. Many have taken the first step. With every additional step you enhance immensely the value of the first."

Ralph Waldo Emerson

- A set of European History personally signed by their previous owner, Arnold Toynbee (If you're into history you will know who he is);

- Lots of volumes on Churchill and Kennedy;

- A Gutenberg Bible (well, maybe one day!)

My point is that, although we all have a spending Achilles heel, if we don't at least try to control it, we can run the risk of sabotaging these our best laid plans...

KNOW WHERE YOU ARE AT

"Be sure you know the condition of your flocks, give careful attention to your herds; for riches do not endure forever..."[15]

The foundation of frugality is, of course, the household budget. If you hate that word... get over it! Without one you are kidding yourself.

I write not as one who is a keen budgeter. For many years I had a belief that budgets were for everybody else but me. Budgets are for the accountant types, satirised in many Monty Python skits as being "numbers people" who are boring, banal and colourless. But I… I am adventurous, spontaneous, and boundary-less. I hate being hemmed in and budgets are financial bars that imprison the poet soul!

Such emotional drivel enabled me to sidestep the demands of a rigorous financial control system… but only for so long. Sooner or later I had to confront what it was I didn't like about this necessary, yet onerous, practice. The fact was that, in my situation, I was afraid, and the foundation of my fear was all about discovering reality. Intuitively I had a sense that my financial world was not improving and I knew that if I put pen to paper and worked out where the money was going, I would have to make some changes. So for me it was easier to live in a false world than face the facts.

Budgets, you see, define reality rather than what we want to be real. They are fantasy-destroying documents. Without their truth and discipline we can think that all is well when in fact the end is nigh. A true budget forces decisions, and decisions are the stuff upon which wealth is built. They are necessary no matter where you are on the continuum of financial independence. In fact, the wealthier someone is, the greater the chances that he or she has a budget.

Another reason why people don't budget is that they simply don't like maths. Numbers bamboozle, and so it seems a lot easier to fly by the seat of one's pants rather than commit pen to paper. Of course, the huge array of sophisticated books on this subject doesn't help. A 300-page tome on 'simple money management' does little to engender confidence within the heart of the "I only got 20% for maths in high school" individual.

So take it from me - all you need is a piece of paper and a pen. Write down all the money that comes in [A], write down all the money that goes out [B], subtract B from A and you should have a positive number here. If you don't - start cutting costs immediately. There... and if you've just followed my advice, you have saved yourself at least $20 on one of those jargon filled, pretentious, patronising, paperbacks!

CHAPTER 5

DANCING WITHOUT DEBT

"THE BORROWER IS SERVANT TO THE LENDER."[16]

Debt has become a way of life. A trusted friend, a needed companion, someone who is always there helping us from crisis to crisis and requiring nothing from us but our interest!

What's more, in today's world, short-term debt opportunities abound. They flirt shamelessly with us from billboards and peep at us from the latest magazine. They don't play hard to get and promise more pleasure with each increase of our credit limit. Only pay the minimum required, they whisper, and gullibly we agree, smiling at our good fortune - another month survived.

Not only that, but the finance companies keep producing pretty coloured cards: green, blue, gold, platinum and even black. Pay yours on time and these kindly souls are likely to double your debit limit and then call it credit limit, all for your convenience. It's so easy to pay as well, because we only have to pay the small figure at the bottom of the account, and not the big one at the top.

Have you ever wondered how long it takes to pay off a card by only paying the minimum required? Let's say your debt is $5,000. The minimum required is usually 2% of the unpaid balance with the debt costing somewhere between 18 - 22% interest. If you never used the card again and continued to pay this 'required amount', it would be 32 years and seven months until the card was clear! On the other hand, if you were to deposit that same $5,000 into a savings account, compounding at 10% for the same length of time, you would have $12,968.71 [$5,000 (1.10) ^10 (assuming interest is paid yearly) = $12,968.71 less $5,000 deposit - $7,968.71 interest] in the bank. It really does matter what side of the interest equation we are on.

"THE PHILOSOPHY OF THE RICH VERSUS THE PHILOSOPHY OF THE POOR IS THIS; THE RICH INVEST THEIR MONEY AND SPEND WHAT IS LEFT, THE POOR SPEND THEIR MONEY AND INVEST WHAT IS LEFT."

JIM ROHN

"Maybe death and taxes are inevitable, but death doesn't get worse every time Congress meets."

Joan Welsh

Henry Ward Beecher stated that debt "gnaws at a man's substance with invisible teeth". It erodes not just who he is and what he has, but what he could be and what he could have.

Compare, for example, two couples living next door to each other in an inner city townhouse.

- COUPLE #1

...enjoy life and enjoy spending and they haven't, as a result, been able to save a deposit so they are renting at $180 a week. They have also just purchased a new sports car worth $40,000 with monthly repayments of $857.59 [Loan period = 5 years. Interest Rate = 10.10% fixed].

- COUPLE #2

...are on exactly the same income but have been able to save $15,000 and use this as a deposit on their $120,000 townhouse. Their older second-hand car works well, so they are putting their entire surplus into their 20-year mortgage. Repayments required are $772.00 but they have increased them to $1,577.00 [Interest Rate = 6.32% fixed. The loan is reduced to 6.11 years]. So both couples are spending the same amount per month for vehicle and housing. The difference between them is clearly seen five years down the track.

Let's say the housing market has only appreciated 5% annually.

- COUPLE #1

  ...only have a vehicle worth between $18,000 - $20,000.

- COUPLE #2

  ...now have a mortgage upon which they owe$32,966 whilst their home in turn is now worth $152,000.

In a five-year period, the disparity between the two couples is $119,034 equity on house and a car worth $18,000 to $20,000. [These figures are purely subjective to the above-mentioned examples; many variables have been assumed for the purposes of illustration, eg. fixed interest rates, economic conditions. It is recommended that each person seeks professional advice before engaging in investments activities.]

WHY DEBT IS SO WONDERFUL

The temptation of debt is indeed a force to be reckoned with. I once had in my possession a small book put out by Debtors Anonymous[17], which listed many reasons why we find debt so attractive. Although I can no longer find the book (maybe it was repossessed) the reasons still ring true today.

1. WHEN THE GOING GETS TOUGH THE TOUGH GO SHOPPING

2. I'M ENTITLED

For some reason - indeed, as it appears, any reason - we will discover ways to psychologically con ourselves into justifying our debt levels. "I am entitled because… I just got married, I just got divorced, I just got a raise, I just got fired, my dog had puppies, I have four small children, life is tough, it's a beautiful day, it's not a beautiful day, etc. etc."

3. EGO

When our self-esteem is flimsy, the opinion of others becomes one of the major motivating forces of our life. What people think of us - we often believe - is based very much on image - the car we drive, the house we live in, the clothes we wear. And so we spend, not on what we need but because we feel the need to be needed.

4. THE BIG FIX

It is easy to allow yourself to get into debt when you are holding out for a big fix. Maybe you are expecting a raise in pay, the death of a rich relative or perhaps that strange invention you came up with several years ago to be picked up and earn you a million dollars.

5. I'M A SPECIAL CASE

Yes it's true that debt can be a problem and for the majority of the people, for the majority of the time, it should be kept under control. But you see, I'm a special case. I'm an actor, small business owner, policeman, unemployed.

I'm a waiter, musician. I'm a butcher, a baker, a candlestick maker...

The time honoured principle is still valid today ...borrow for appreciating assets, don't for depreciating ones. Noel Whittaker in his book on financial management[18] points out there are some exceptions to this rule when, for example, one buys a swimming pool for the home in autumn on a one-year fixed repayment scheme. The advantage of winter prices works out considerably more than the interest cost over the loan term. Yet such exceptions are just that... exceptions.

In general, debt for consumer goods is just not worth it, and it's not worth it for a whole bunch of reasons:

Firstly, as the Proverb at the beginning of this chapter points out, debt enslaves a person. Not only to the one to whom money has been loaned, but also to the pressure of earning. It is not unusual for couples to have between two and four different jobs collectively. They will tell you they need to do so in order to get by, but when we examine what 'getting by' means, we discover it is purely because of a high debt level, the result of unnecessary goods that have been purchased as a reward for all the hard work… and so the cycle continues.

The bumper sticker got it right, "I owe, I owe, so off to work I go."

Such pressure undermines the joy of life which is discovered through many pursuits, chief amongst them giving and helping others. High debt levels means there is very little time or money left over for anybody else. I don't know about you but I think I can get by without the latest model flat screen TV, but I can't get by without time with my kids, spontaneity in my life, fun in my marriage and a sense of peace at the closing of each day.

SO HOW DO I ESCAPE?

The financial plan we discussed in chapter 3 should include some specifics in this area. Here are a few ideas:

Number 1 - Pay Off Debt Systematically

"Too many people spend money they haven't earned, to buy things they don't want, to impress people they don't like."

Will Rogers

"IF YOU WANT
TO EARN MORE
THAN YOU GET,
YOU NEED TO BE
WORTH MORE
THAN YOU ARE
PAID."

NAPOLEON HILL

List all your debts from smallest to largest. Whilst making all the regular payments, focus your energy on getting rid of the smallest one on the list. When this is done, apply that payment to the next on the list, and so on and so forth.

Number 2 - Lock Away Your Credit Cards

No point reducing debt on one hand while spending continues on the other. If locking away doesn't work for you then conduct a credit card funeral service, cremating or burying as soon as possible.

Number 3 - Downsize

Contentment is not having what you want but wanting what you have. There are discontented billionaires and happy-go-lucky, well contented tramps. Joy in life is not based on what you have, but on how you think about what you have. The fun of owning a pre-loved car, debt free, exceeds that of the new model with monthly repayments stretching multiple years into the future.

Sometimes major surgery is required. Moving to a smaller home or cheaper suburb, getting rid of the boat that is hardly used. Remember, we are not saying these things are wrong, merely that the timing of their purchase should be based on increased wealth, not increased debt.

Number 4 - The Garage Sale

Get rid of clutter. Sell what you can and use the cash to pay off debt. Periodically we have a garage sale... it's amazing how much junk builds up which can be turned back into money.

There has been a resurgence as well in shops selling pre-loved clothes. Small boutiques will on sell, for a small commission, that nice outfit you never wear any more, or the kids' good clothes that have been outgrown. Don't let them sit in the wardrobe or the cardboard box in the attic when they could be paying off your debts.

Number 5 - Eat Out Less

I do a great Bolognese, complete with my own secret sauce, garlic, mushrooms and red wine. Yet it only costs $8 to feed my family of five. Simple fish and chips for all of us costs at least $15, McDonald's comes in at $16, Chinese at $33, Indian at $40 and these are all on the cheaper end of the scale. If you live in America, the cost of eating out is a lot less, but money can still be saved by remaining vigilant in this area.

Number 6 - Don't Go Crazy at Christmas

My inlaws are wonderful people but their spending Achilles heel used to be birthdays and Christmas. They have been known to blow hundreds of dollars, which they couldn't afford, on their family. (Please note if my inlaws are reading this, I don't want you to stop giving! Just set a realistic limit and stick to it.) We must not let the celebration of the season demolish our financial sense.

In fact, most families would appreciate a decent inheritance twenty years down the track more than the top of the range gizmo today.

Number 7 - Use the Library

Many people spend more than $10 a week on magazines and newspapers. $10 they don't have to spend as the local library will probably have both for your reading pleasure. I love to read the papers, especially on Saturday. These include the Financial Australian, Weekend Australian and Saturday West Australian (total cost $4.00). So I visit a coffee shop that has all three and invest half of my savings on a cappuccino.

The library is even better than the coffee shop. The children love it and now that videos are available there as well, the trip is even more worthwhile.

If you normally buy one children's book a month for let's say $15.00 and rent one video at $5.00, there is a yearly saving of $240.

Number 8 - Don't Carry a Lot of Cash

The more money you carry around, the more likely you are to spend it. There is something about the crisp $50 bill in your pocket. It is so available, so willing. It is not long before it has worked its magic and exchanged itself for unwanted goods or services.

On the other hand, it is easy to resist the temptation to spend when purchasing is a physical impossibility.

Number 9 - Watch Out for Addictive Behaviour

If you are an addictive personality, get help. There is no surer path to financial ruin than enforced spending, driven by an addictive psyche. I am not just speaking of the endemic drug problem. Gambling and sexuality have their fair share of victims as well. I have only gambled once and, in hindsight, I am glad I did not win.

My best friend's sister worked for the CEO of a large company. One of his side lines was horse racing and one day he announced to the young lady that he had a horse running in a country race that afternoon. "If you want to make some money", he suggested, "put a dollar or two on my horse. We have it all organised. It will win." The girl phoned her brother, who phoned me. "It's a sure thing", he said, and I had to agree as the rumour could be sourced right back to, pardon the pun, the horse's mouth... so I took all my savings and put them on the horse's nose. $200 to win at odds of 15 to 1. Later that day, I picked up my fiance. My plan was to keep quiet, listen to the race on the radio as we were driving along, then announce to my bride-to-be that we were $3,000 better off thanks to my brilliance. The horse ran last. My stomach sank and I decided that the discretion and valour quote was entirely appropriate.

Some are addicted to pornography and yield their cash to the insistence of libido. The Book of Proverbs specifically targets this area; it warns about the dangers of adultery and prostitution when it says, "Keep to a path far from her. Do not go near the door of her house... lest strangers feast on your wealth and your toil enrich another man's house."[19]

"We must all suffer from one of two pains - the pain of discipline or the pain of regret. The difference is, the pain of discipline weighs ounces while the pain of regret weighs tons."

Jim Rohn

"Wall Street is the only place to which people ride in a Rolls Royce to get advice from those who take the subway."

"The prostitute reduces you to a loaf of bread and the adulterous preys upon your very life."[20]

It seems that morality is not only good for the soul but is also a necessary ally on the road to wealth as well.

Number 10 - Going Guarantor

If it's not good to have your own debts, it's even worse to guarantee someone else's. Don't allow the persuasion of a friend, or for that matter a partner, to cause you to sign something that you either don't understand or couldn't afford if things don't work out. If a guarantee is required because the venture is risky, or the figures don't add up, then wisdom would say run!

There are of course exceptions to this rule. Many banks require directors of public and private companies to sign directors' guarantees on bank loans held in the company's name. This can often be required, regardless of the strength of the balance sheet. In such cases the primary motive is to make sure the directors are personally liable for the decisions they make. The problem with going guarantor in most situations is that you are liable for all debt even though you are not the one making the decisions. You have responsibility but not authority. You have the risk but not the profit. The downside, but not the upside.

The other obvious exception is where parents help their children in the purchase of their first home. Normally, in such cases, banks are reluctant to go ahead with the eighteen-year-old who has no credit history, unless they have some extra names on the document. Yet, this too is highly negotiable. The bottom line is most lenders will try to get as much security as they can.

The Jewish culture continually reinforced the importance of debt elimination through the custom of Sabbath years and jubilee. In short, these were certain times when all debts were cancelled. Debt, although seen as necessary in the purchase of land and housing, was viewed as episodic rather than permanent.

Today, many of us have been brought up with a culture that embodies debt as lifestyle. The individual who is debt free is unusual. Indeed, many whose goal is to pay off the debts are motivated purely because this allows them to borrow again. So, although debt can be used creatively and wisely in building up an impressive property portfolio, the concept that debt should be a way of life, as culturally normal, should be challenged.

The dance of the debt-free is one of great joy and easy movement; the sooner we can get on the floor, the better.

CHAPTER 6

SIDESTEPPING THE SHARKS

"A SIMPLE MIND BELIEVES ANYTHING BUT A PRUDENT MAN GIVES THOUGHT TO HIS STEPS."[21]

When money is to be made the water teems with monsters from the deep. Indeed, the higher the potential pay-off, the greater the chance that the unsuspecting investor will become another expendable extra in the reddening waters of Jaws 5.

What is even more interesting is that the victim becomes as frenzied as the foe. As potential profit margins grow so it seems brain cells die. Smart people do stupid things when a quick buck is to be made. If one is to be wealthy, one must be astute as well.

It could be argued that the greedy deserve all that they get. Yet often the victims of con men and shucksters are the compassionate, the caring or simply the naive. Add to this the fact that there are varieties of shark as well. From the terrifying Great White whose whole purpose in life is to get you, to, as the name suggests, the helpful Grey Nurse, who accidentally bites your leg off.

In other words we can all lose money to both the bad dealers and the bad deals. The point is the Wealthy Achiever makes himself fully aware of the risks, never allowing optimism to run away from reality. The ability to say no is as important as the ability to say yes.

Anyone who has been out of school more than 10 years has seen their share of deals come and go. With age, hopefully there comes greater discernment. Yet, unfortunately, this is not always the case. In my role as Pastor of a church I have the opportunity to see first hand the damage that can be done through believing that everyone we deal with is well intentioned. In fact, churches are often targeted by the more unscrupulous as they are rich feeding grounds of compassionate and trusting people. Their modus operandi seems to be, attend for a few weeks, get to know as many people as possible and then begin to share with carefully selected targets their huge need for extra cash because of:

A a new orphanage they are building in India.

B a great invention which God has given them which will generate millions of dollars in revenue for the local church.

C some great investment property in a place far, far away, but if you act now before anyone else knows about it, you will be richly rewarded.

There are of course, valid investment opportunities in property and inventions, as well as highly effective orphanages in India. The important thing is, to check out the claims.

I know of one farmer who was greatly generous and gave tens of thousands of dollars, over many years, to an institution for poor children in a third world country, only to discover that the whole thing was a scam, fabricated by photos and letters. It was only when he decided to turn up for a surprise visit that he discovered the truth.

So how are we to protect ourself against such plots?

1. STAY EMOTIONALLY DETACHED

The old adage puts it thus; "There is none so blind as though as those who will not see." When we want something to be true, for us it is true. If we think the property is unique and we really want to buy it then we tend to easily discount any evidence that suggests that it is over-priced.

In life we tend to see what we are looking for. It was William Blake who wrote, "we see not with but through the eye." We see with our brain. Everything we see has a part of us connected to it. The critical individual will always see things to criticise. The jealous will see things to envy and the pessimist will always have something to complain about. Their vision is selective because in their case desire creates

"A STUDY OF ECONOMICS REVEALS THAT THE BEST TIME TO BUY ANYTHING IS USUALLY LAST YEAR."

"MONEY DOESN'T

GROW ON TREES

AND IF IT DID

SOMEONE ELSE

WOULD OWN THE

ORCHARD."

reality. We must, therefore, train ourselves to remain objective.

2. TALK TO OTHER PEOPLE

Where we have blind spots, others do not. Therefore it is always good to ask several significant others: people who have no agenda and people who will be frank. One of the warning signs of a bad investment opportunity is when the person who is offering this amazing opportunity to you, adds the caveat, "Don't tell anybody else about this."

The financial abuser and sexual abuser are the same in this regard. They know that once word gets out, their exploitation will be seen for what it really is and the prey will escape.

3. DON'T GO AGAINST YOUR GUT

Intuition is a powerful, yet under-trusted guide in such matters. If your head is saying, 'this looks like a good deal', but there is something on the inside that makes you feel uncomfortable, especially if this is echoed by a spouse or trusted friend, then begin to back away. You lose nothing by saying "No" but you could lose everything by saying "Yes". I have heard too many stories of people who have lost it all, who recounted afterwards how they had a niggling doubt, a strange, almost nauseating feeling in the pit of their stomach, which was pacified momentarily by the suave and soft words of the deal maker.

4. BEWARE OF "SPIN"

The less validity something has the more one has to hype it to get a sale. We live in an age when the medium is the message: where packaging sells and people judge from the graphics. In political circles, making a bad thing sound good is called "spin" and the 'spin-doctors' work their art furiously in order to get their candidate elected. When something looks too good, when everything is perfect, when the artwork is brilliant and the hype is world-class, it means, more often than not, that the core may be suspect.

I know of one investor who was looking seriously at buying a franchise in the first attempt to expand America's National Football League into Europe. He liked what he saw and was going to go ahead with the deal until he was invited to attend a special banquet, along with other potential investors of different European franchises. He remarked how it was a tremendous evening, no expense spared. And then at the end of the night, the spotlight fell on different tables and the announcer's voice was heard asking the questions, "Is London in? Is Paris in? Is Berlin in?" and with each question a potential investor waved, then stood indicating that a decision had been made. When it came time for his turn, he declined, commenting afterwards that any deal that needed that much pressure, placing the individual under great embarrassment if they said no, must not be a good deal... the 'spin' was too strong. The resulting expansion failed, yet one Wealthy Achiever continued on his way, capital intact.

5. ASK TOUGH QUESTIONS

With every opportunity there are always many questions that must be asked. I always get suspicious when the person making the offer is using technical jargon accompanied by complex charts, placing me in a situation where I feel foolish if I ask questions. Often this is done deliberately. In a good deal, questions are encouraged. In a bad one the superficial ones are answered, the fundamental ones are laughed off, dismissed or avoided.

So ask away. It is a lot better to look the fool before the deal is struck than to obviously be one afterwards.

"A SMALL SHARE

IN A GOOD

PROPERTY IS

BETTER THAN

100% OF A WHITE

ELEPHANT."

CHAPTER 7

ACQUIRING ASSETS, INVESTIGATING INVESTMENTS AND EXPOSING EXPENSES

"DEVELOP YOUR BUSINESS FIRST
BEFORE BUILDING YOUR
HOUSE."[22]

The secrets of wealth have moved from the general to the specific. The larger bowl to the smaller one, each one relying on the previous for its own viability. Our plan controls our spending, eradicates our debt so that we have money left over... savings.

The secret of wealth, however, is not just creating surplus but using it wisely. We must not allow it to simply sit and earn minimum interest. We must put it to work. The difference between the rich and poor is that the poor work for money, but the rich make sure money works for them. Each dollar is like a labourer. The more I have at my disposal, the more can be accomplished. In the early stages they work hard and reproduce slowly, but soon, like rabbits they multiply. And as a result greater tasks can be accomplished with increased rapidity.

So what work is the best work? Not that which is so strenuous that our labourers burn out on high return yet high risk projects. And not the easy road either where they lie on the beach sunning themselves at 2 or 3%. Somewhere between these extremes is the middle ground, where good returns and good growth are both discovered. Solid income-producing assets must be found and invested in.

An investment must generate an income or return. This is the meaning of the word. The

Oxford Dictionary defines the verb "to invest" as, "To expend (money, effort) in something from which a return or profit is expected, esp. in the purchase of property, shares, etc. for the sake of the interest, dividends or profits accruing from them."[23]

Martin Hawes defines it even further when he says, "An investment must carry a return. For something to be an investment there has to be an expected income from it. This income is generated by the investment assets; it is not from a change in value of the investment itself."[24]

Once we understand this, we begin to realise that many so-called investments are not investments at all. They should be more correctly called speculations. Oxford again defines speculation as a "Risky enterprise, in the hope of considerable gain; gamble." Art or antiques, vintage cars or 1¢ shares on the stock market can all be speculative. High returns may be made, but on the other hand... In fact, most wise people who speculate do so with a small percentage of their available investment money and do so because the area holds special interest for them. I mean, after all, driving the Mark 2 Jaguar is a lot more fun than checking up on the investment unit. Just don't get upset if the Jag ends up costing you money.

Now obviously anyone trying to get hold of your money does not call a speculation a speculation. The word is always 'invest' because everyone knows that investments are wise, stable and solid, whilst speculations are the stuff of fast talking entrepreneurs and rip-off merchants. Whilst these caricatures are not always fair, it is important that we know what we are getting into. If you want to speculate, speculate, but don't call it an investment.

When seen in this light, there are only three major investment areas:

Number 1 - Interest Bearing Deposits

Number 2 - Property (residential, commercial; land is only an investment if income is being earned, i.e. leased for cattle raising etc.)

Number 3 - Owning a business, either totally or in part.

There are many different investment vehicles within each of these areas with fancy names

"It is difficult to save money when your neighbours keep buying things you can't afford."

"THE EASIEST

WAY TO MAKE A

MILLION DOLLARS

IS TO START WITH

$900,000."

and impressive jargon, like Superannuation Funds, Unit Trusts, Share Index Funds, Bank Bills, Group Investment Funds, Debenture Stocks, etc. etc. They are merely approaching the purchasing and managing of property or businesses as a group of investors, usually with a manager. In this way, you can own a small part of the major office block and get your money out quickly if you need to. It requires less start-up capital than direct investing, but there are extra fees as well.

WHY YOUR HOUSE IS NOT AN ASSET

It all depends on how you define asset. Traditionally an asset is anything you have that can be sold to pay off debts. Well, this could include almost anything and indeed when we usually work out our net worth we add up everything we own. We don't want to depress ourselves, so normally the value written down takes it for granted that demand will be very high for all our junk. After all, who wouldn't want to pay $100 for the espresso machine that cost $120 five years ago? Once a total is reached, all debt is deducted and the amount left is net worth. Now, in reality, if we had to sell, the amount realised would be far less. But let's not worry about such insignificant details right now.

If your list is anything like mine, most of what I have put down under assets are non-income producing; books, clothes, furniture - while some actually cost money to keep them. Take, for example, the family home. We have always been told that our house is our most important asset, but what type of asset is it? Does it create income? Is it neutral? Or does it actually cost us? Do we find that by owning our own home, money is being earned? Or does it still take cash out of our pocket? The truth is that even if we own our home outright, repairs and rates still mean that this asset costs. Certainly, it costs less than renting yet it is not income-producing. The same could be said for the car and household appliances. Although we don't list them under expenses they can be expensive. Now, technically, these things are still assets but they are neutral at best. They do not put money directly into our pocket.

As we have already seen, buying our own home is a wise thing to do but it is not the only thing to do. We must also starting adding assets that create a positive cash flow. The point of the

Proverb at the beginning of the chapter is just this - fields create income, our house and other so-called assets don't.

POSITIVE ASSETS

A positive asset is where money is created. Money, either by appreciation that can be utilised, or income production. Or best of all - both. Here are some things that fit our definition.

Number 1 - Investment Property

What is great about investment property is that not only do you have a renter helping you pay for it as well as the appreciation within the housing market, but also in most cases, tax benefits as well. Many times the net cost is minimal, even when the mortgage is at its highest. Add to this the fact that your money is leveraged because you gain appreciation on the total value of the property and not just the small amount you used as a deposit.

Robert Kiyosaki in his book, If you Want to be Rich and Happy, Don't Go to School[25], tells of an experience he had which clearly shows the difference between how consumers and wealth achievers think.

He was looking through an apartment complex with a view to investing. As he was touring various units, he noticed they all had expensive stereos or large screen TVs ranging in price from US$800 - US$8,000. He ran the numbers in his head and realised that although he could afford to buy the apartment he could not afford to buy the stereos. The renter and the taxman would help in the purchase of the unit, which would then appreciate in value. While no one would help with the purchase of the expensive stereo, which would then depreciate. In this case the apartment is the real asset, the stereo the bogus one.

Number 2 - Shares

Shares can be excellent assets both in earning (the dividend) and in appreciation, depending on the company selected and the state of the market. For many, those conditions make share investment more difficult to get right than property. The majority on the road to wealth use either property or the share market as their respective vehicles. Property is easier to understand but the share market should not be underestimated in its ability to produce returns. Yet enter either one hastily and painful lessons will be learned.

My own forays into the share market have been built upon an amazing amount of ignorance and usually encouraged by rumour. My first experience was to speculate in a small stock in a company that had produced an experimental engine. Shares were about 40¢ when I heard that a secret deal, very hush hush, was about to be signed with a major automobile maker. How I heard about it, I cannot remember now but I was sure I was onto privileged and, of course, correct information. I talked a friend of mine into coming up with half the money and together we decided to sink a massive $500 into the fledgling company. (On my income in 1980, the only correct word that could be used here is the word MASSIVE!)

I left the details of actually purchasing the shares to my friend, who took three days to get to a broker and put in the order. In the meantime, the price had soared to $1.69. We bought in at the highest recorded sale upon which the tide retreated as quickly as it had come in. Three years later I finally sold my holdings for 22¢ a share.

The morals of the story are:

A Don't speculate unless you are happy to lose it all.

B Don't believe the whispered rumour; "A friend of mine down the pub told me..."

C Don't let your friend buy for you... when he gets around to it.

BUY QUALITY

Martin Hawes defines "quality investment" as "one with good sustainable income which is likely to grow". In other words, the quality of an investment is linked to its income generation rather than its possible appreciation. Which, if you think about it, will happen if the income being earned is going up. In short, quality is about desirability. Desirability in real estate has mostly to do with location and the solidness of the property. Desirability in the share market

"IF THE INVESTMENT WATERS ARE MUDDIED, DON'T JUMP IN."

"THE FIRST RULE

OF INVESTING IS

NOT TO LOSE THE

PRINCIPAL. THE

SECOND RULE IS

NOT TO FORGET

THE FIRST RULE."

has to do with businesses that have good leadership and management skills, within stable industries and are progressive in nature.

Quality cannot mean, "I really like it." Now you may have good taste that accurately reflects the tastes of the general buying public, but there again you might be weird! "That group of units next to the airport, miles from public transport, has got a lovely garden." Or, "those shares will be great because that company has a monopoly - they're the only ones left making asbestos cladding." So make sure you have some kind of objective basis for deciding quality, something a bit more stringent than the graphic design of the prospectus.

So, let us look at some of the major differences between investing in property and investing in the share market.

Number 1 - A good share has a greater potential for gain

The overall trend in the stock market is a lot higher than the housing market. Returns of 20%+ are common, whereas in property they are the exception.

Number 2 - You can get out of shares quicker than you can get out of property

Shares are more liquid. A phone call today to your broker, and you can be out of the market within minutes. Selling a house is a totally different proposition.

Number 3 - Share prices are more volatile

This is the corollary of the previous point. Panic selling can take place far easier in the share market with resulting major falls in a day. It is a lot harder to be panic driven when it take four to twelve weeks or longer to sell a house.

Number 4 - You always know what your shares are worth

Every day the paper lets you know how well (or how badly) you are doing. In the property market you never really know until the cheque is in the bank.

Number 5 - You cannot enhance the price of shares

There is not much you can do to increase the value of your shares unless you happen to be the managing director of the company in question. Yet, a little landscaping, painting, cleaning or renovating can add real value to your home or investment property.

Number 6 - It is easier to borrow against property

This is due to its greater stability. One can borrow against it for the next property or investment a lot easier than one can with shares.

Number 7 - Income from shares and property can have different tax advantages

Income from shares may already have tax paid on it (franked dividends). Property can be negatively geared and depending upon your own tax situation may prove more advantageous than other alternatives.

Number 8 - Property is more permanent

Companies can come and go; even the best of them can cease to exist, through bad management, legal complications or diminishing markets. The house, on the other hand, unless it is starring as a prop in the film Twister, will probably still be around in a hundred years' time - certainly the land will be.

Number 9 - Property has ongoing costs

Shares don't cost you once you own them, unless you are buying and selling every day in which case your profit will dwindle as the brokers take their fee at each transaction.

Property, on the other hand, has regular costs, such as maintenance, management and rates. Property can also be trashed by a bad tenant or sit vacant between leases.

Stocks and property are not, of course, the only income-producing assets. There are other things such as royalties for intellectual property (books, articles, songs or inventions), managed funds (investing in property, shares, insurance bonds or equity trusts), or businesses that don't require your day-to-day presence.

The secret is to start planting the field. The sooner money starts to work for you rather than the other way around, the quicker financial independence will be realised.

CHAPTER 8

GROWING WITH GENEROSITY

"THE WORLD OF THE GENEROUS GROWS LARGER AND LARGER. THE WORLD OF THE STINGY GETS SMALLER AND SMALLER."[26]

Most people don't think of generosity as being part of the process of wealth creation… out of everything we have looked at, it is the hardest to get one's head around. Not in the sense of wanting to be generous or considering whether generosity is a good or bad thing, but in the sense of understanding how it is connected with wealth creation.

However, Wealthy Achievers understand the importance of this intangible. In a concrete world, tangibility is almost synonymous with validity and yet wisdom would not only point out that one of the great purposes of prosperity is generosity, but also that it is also inextricably involved in the process of wealth creation itself.

There are a variety of reasons for this and, when taken together, they become compelling.

Number 1 - Generosity Maintains Perspective

Goals which are no bigger than ourselves or our immediate family lack energy, meaning and true fulfilment; a truth that is often lost in the weekly hustle and bustle of earning, spending and saving. It is easy to begin to think that we ourselves are the sole purpose of our quest for financial independence.

Small ambitions and selfish goals have no lasting power and, although the life based on them may grow in financial net worth, it is also, at the same time, getting "smaller and smaller". One of the reasons that generosity

"THERE ARE TWO TYPES OF ECONOMISTS; THOSE WHO DON'T KNOW THE FUTURE AND THOSE THAT DON'T KNOW THAT THEY DON'T KNOW THE FUTURE."

"THE BIG PRINT

GIVETH, AND THE

SMALL PRINT

TAKETH AWAY."

must be practised from the beginning is to help us keep our eyes on that which is really important. The end rather than the means. Enhancing lives rather than gathering funds. Helping others rather than just helping ourselves.

Number 2 - Generosity Keeps us the Master

Jesus would often speak about the "deceitfulness of riches"[27]. Money has this power to muddy our vision, to pull us, as Darth Vader would say, "toward the dark side". Greed grabs the soul slowly, one longing at a time. Materialism becomes a dominant reality, one asset at a time. Slowly money becomes the master as it weaves its way into our heart creating a one-way love affair, which the Bible declares is, "the root of all evil".

The habit of generosity, however, slashes this money-monster where he is the most vulnerable. You think you're the boss? Okay, I'll give you away. Regular acts of generosity break the power of greed's hold. The reason many people struggle when churches and non-profits talk about giving money is not that they have a problem with what these respective organisations are doing. (In my experience, the majority of such organisations are healthy and accountable; they are stretching every dollar to the max and providing help, both spiritual and practical. In a society where the darkness and despair is growing year by year, they are in many cases the only rays of light.) No, people get upset about money when money has got too tight of a grip on them. There is nothing like the challenge of generosity to show us where our hearts really are.

Number 3 - Generosity Produces Dividends

If it is true that riches deceive and stinginess narrows vision, then it must also be true that generosity keeps us clear-eyed and puts us in a place where we can view a broader horizon. Here, of course, is a hook where all you tangibility-buffs can hang your coat.

Generosity will help me see things that the stingy will miss. Opportunities will be spotted, relationships will be formed, my world grows bigger and, as a result, the dividends that generosity pays will not just be measured with increased self-esteem or the gratefulness of society, but with a real growth in the bottom line as well.

I am convinced that if you took two people on the pathway to wealth, both of whom diligently applied the principles contained in this volume, yet one fudged this last principle and the other did not, you would discover, in the long run, the generous individual would not just be better off in terms of spiritual health and emotional vitality, but also in terms of net worth as well.

The maxim continues to hold true, "give and it shall be given to you"[28].

Number 4 - Generosity Dissuades Pride

There has been a connection throughout history between money and arrogance, between riches and snobbishness, between the millionaire and the egocentric. Now some of this, to be sure, is perception. I remember a friend of mine who was told when he was growing up not to spend time with a certain family who had money because they were snobs. Yet when he got to know them, he quickly realised this was not the case at all. His family were in fact the snobs who judged people through the prism of their own envy.

Yet, it does make sense that the "haves" will probably have more of a battle with pride than the "have-nots"; those who are succeeding financially than the declared bankrupts. I am speaking in general terms but certainly in my experience, high-mindedness and hubris seem to increase as income rises. This is certainly true amongst the image conscious, high cash flow, yet debt-ridden members of society. The principle of generosity, however, inoculates the heart against the ravages of pride. It keeps you down to earth and mindful of the responsibilities as well as the privileges that financial independence brings.

Again, like the previous point, this will actually have an effect on the bottom line. Another Proverb declares, "Pride comes before a fall".[29] The reason this is true is that pride creates its own problems. It is less cautious and trusts its own ability more than it should. Egotistical myopia takes over and, as a result, stupid decisions are made.

The proud individual also finds that everyone around him, or her, is secretly hoping that things will go wrong. The humble, generous, wealthy individual discovers that colleagues, employees and even competitors have a soft spot for them. There is almost a community sense of encouragement - people want you to do well. The stingy and proud find that the opposite is the case and will often be undone because of enemies that have been created along the way. The generous are certainly not free from problems, but their paths are not nearly so cluttered.

Number 5 - Generosity Releases Favour

Whether you call it "Sowing and Reaping", "Giving and Receiving", the "Golden Rule" or the "Law of Attraction", I firmly believe that the favour of God is upon those who are big-hearted enough to share what they have. When we realise we are blessed in order to be a blessing, then there is a sense of travelling with supernatural wind beneath our wings.

This truth has become obvious even to secular commentators. Writers such as Robert Kiyosaki and Anthony Robbins - who, as far as I am aware, are not Bible-carrying Christians - teach in their material the principle of tithing, of giving, of generosity.

Now again, let me reiterate, one should not get serious about generosity only when things are going well financially, any more than the farmer should get serious about sowing only when the barns are full. The habit of generosity is as important on Day 1 as it is on Day 10,000. The only things that will change are the zeros on the end of the donated cheques.

Number 6 - Generosity Tells Me I Have More Than Enough

The wealthy and the debt-ridden are so because they think differently. What we do proceeds from what we believe, and what we believe is the result of our thinking processes and patterns. Robert Kiyosaki in his book, Rich Dad, Poor Dad, points out that the major difference between the wealthy and those who are not is in how they think. Even when neither of them has any money, the wealthy person

"WHEREVER CALCULUS OR HIGHER ALGEBRA IS BROUGHT IN YOU CAN TAKE IT AS A WARNING SIGN THAT THE ADVISOR IS TRYING TO SUBSTITUTE THEORY FOR EXPERIENCE."

"If all persons calling themselves Investment Advisors were piled on top of each other, beginning at the bottom of the Grand Canyon, it probably would be a good idea."

will say, “I am broke”; in other words this is a temporary condition. The poor person will say, “I am poor” which has a ring of permanence to it.

One of the great things that generosity does is affect the way we think. If we are giving something away then it must mean we have more than enough. When we begin to really believe that, we have rewired the brain, so to speak, in such a way that will enhance wealth creation. If we are thinking, on the other hand, that we never have enough, then discontentment and debt will be the only fruit of our thoughts.

The mind is a very powerful thing. Its multiple synaptic connections in three dimensions between billions of neurons, are so designed that what is continually repeated is retained. Neural pathways are etched into the landscape and the more we travel them, the more beaten the track becomes. After a decade of thinking in a certain way, be it positive or negative, we find it almost impossible to re-route the traffic.

This is why, for example, the theories of Wealthy Achievers are reasonably well known, yet practised by few. The neural freeways that declare, "buy it now, pay for it later" or "spenders have more fun than savers" are so clear and compelling that true wisdom to the contrary appears like some dirt track off to the side. We notice it, we hesitate momentarily but we speed on by - it would just be too difficult to slow down, indicate and turn onto a new and unexplored back road.

So I guess this book is an attempt to stand at the intersection and wave madly to the passing traffic in an attempt to convince them that what they really seek is to be discovered here on the quiet lane, rather than on the frenzied freeway - to try to persuade in the face of media-driven myths. Yet, I suppose that it has been true throughout history that the right way is not always well trodden, that the voice crying in the wilderness can often be right, whilst the clamour of the culture can be deceiving; that the still small voice utters truth ... whilst the chant of the crowd does not. Or, as Jesus put it, "broad is the way that leads to destruction, but narrow is the way that leads to life".

“I WANT A
ONE-ARMED
ECONOMIST SO
THAT THE GUY
CAN NEVER MAKE
A STATEMENT AND
THEN SAY, ‘ON
THE OTHER
HAND’!”

CHAPTER 9

WHISTLING WHILE YOU WORK

"EVEN A MOSQUITO DOESN'T GET A SLAP ON THE BACK UNTIL HE STARTS WORKING."

Our attitude to hard work is based on our philosophy of work.

Is it to be shirked or savoured? Is rest and relaxation the goal of life or should it simply be the gaining of breath ready for the next job? Should we retire to do nothing or to do something? Is work a means or an end?

Unfortunately today, the value of work has fallen. References to it in popular culture are more pejorative than not. Like the old joke, "How long have you been working for the company?" "Since they threatened to fire me!" Or, as Harry Secombe said in one of the better known Goon Shows, "It was a wonderful sight - three thousand British workmen, three of them working!"

So, is the cause of work to be avoided or advanced? Can we discover meaning at the coalface or only at the beach? Theologically, some have even argued that work is the result of "the fall", of a world gone wrong and, as a result, an unnecessary evil. Heaven then becomes a place of eternal holiday, nothing to do because nothing needs to be done. Whilst this might seem attractive for the first few hundred years, surely the banality of it all and the boredom of each passing moment would make us realise that this would be hell. Like muscles that don't get used we would die of atrophy or, as Ziglar puts it, "We are designed for accomplishment..."

No, Adam had a prelapsarian job. [It's a great word that means before "the fall" and this is my first opportunity in life to use it, so I had to!] He had to tend the garden. The task provided food for his body, mind and soul. The

“THE BITTERNESS

OF POOR QUALITY

REMAINS AFTER

THE SWEETNESS

OF LOW PRICE

FADES AWAY.”

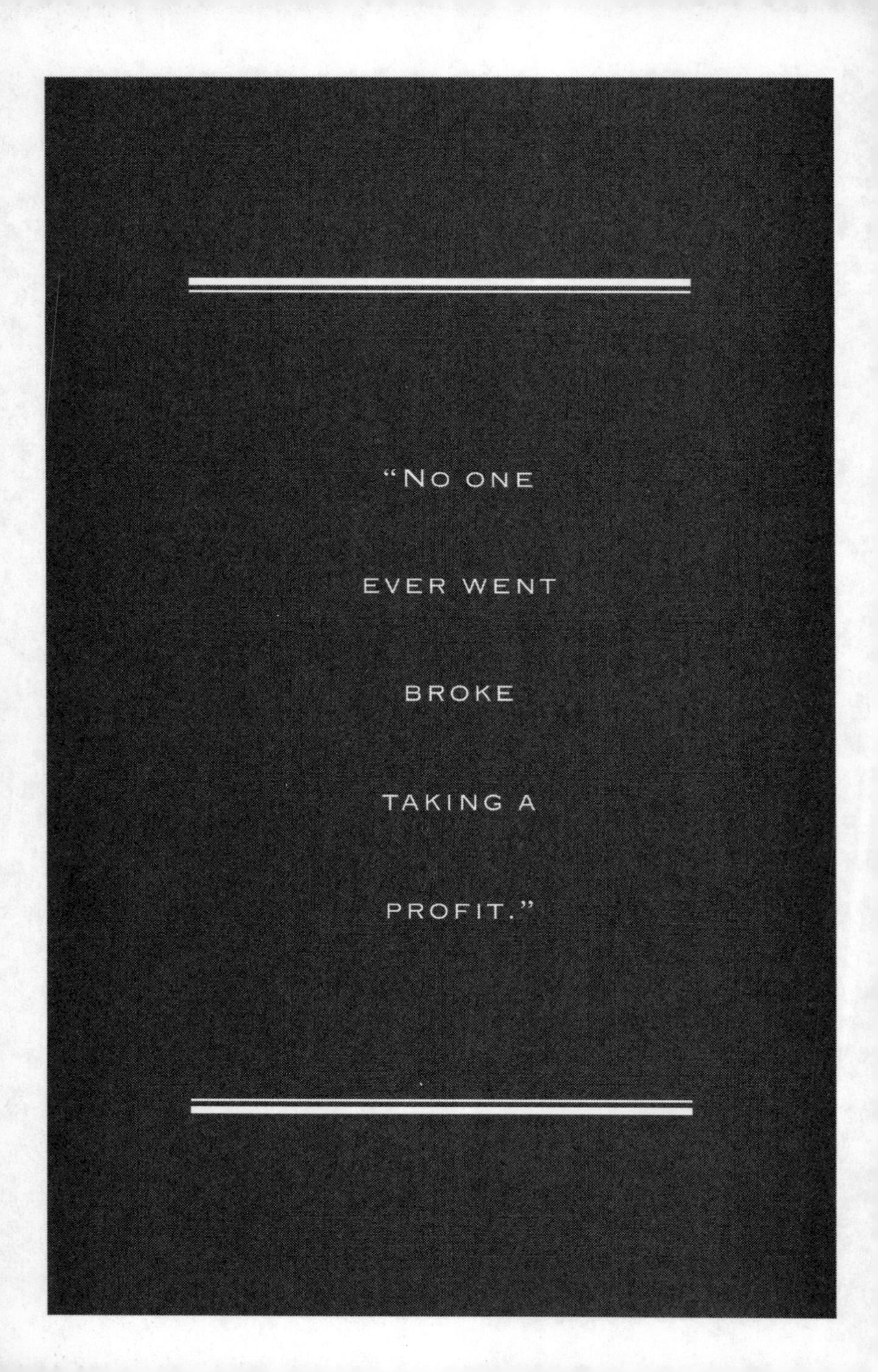
"No one
ever went
broke
taking a
profit."

lazy lose part of themselves as they slumber their lives away. The hard working and the diligent sleep better at night and enjoy their days more.

Diligence is not just about working hard but also speaks to the underlying philosophy of work - what motivates us to do? Is it the pain and punishment that will be ours if we idle away the hours? Is it the tangible reward that comes from applying ourself in the marketplace? For the diligent, it is neither of these.

One authority compares the hard worker to an ant, who, "having no overseer or ruler, yet it stores its provisions."[30] In other words, the ant is self-motivated. Maybe it knows the rewards that will come or the peril of not preparing, yet what moves it onward is genomic. It is, if you like, hot-wired to work hard and long, needing little encouragement or pressure. In the same way, our attitude toward the task should be one that relishes the job and finds working up a sweat part of the meaning and the stuff of life.

Ulysses in Homer's Iliad is captured by Calypso and imprisoned on her island for many years. He has everything he wants except control of his own destiny. He is trapped in a pleasant prison and cries on the beach each night. It is only by leaving the island and travelling onward, facing storms and danger, that he becomes himself again.

Creating wealth requires hard work... not just hard work mind you, but hard work nonetheless. I often hear of people whose goal in life is to become wealthy so they don't have to do anything. I fear that if such a person realises their goal (something that is highly doubtful) they will only discover that where they have arrived is not where they want to be.

We were built to do, to achieve, to make a difference and to put our hands to some great task. Wealth is merely a side product along the way. If it becomes the end, all it means is that better dressed people will attend the funeral, but the life itself would have been wasted.

Let us not also be misguided by thinking that only the important jobs are ones with value. Diligence means doing your best, whatever it is that you are doing - building a wall, cooking a meal or performing a vital operation.

In looking back over my life, I have been involved in working in a host of different situations. I have cooked for Kentucky Fried Chicken [and yes, I still eat it from time to time], cleaned massive tanks at a milk powder plant, put windows in cars on an assembly line, washed dishes, sold advertising, made hay, sold history books - believe it or not - door-to-door, and laboured on building sites. What I do now - pastoring, speaking and writing - has greater meaning in my life than cooking chicken ever did. Yet, the habit of doing a good job then is part of who I am now. Indeed, if my attitude had been one of only working hard in the big tasks, I might still be yet cleaning dishes in some city restaurant.

Charles Schultz, the creator of Peanuts, advised the young cartoonists to, "Do your best cartoon each day." In other words, don't wait until you reach the big time to work your hardest. Work hard now and your future will be far more preferable than if you do not.

I might add that it is important to work in an area that gives us meaning and joy. It might take a while to get there but this should be our goal.

John Clark in his book, The Money or Your Life[31], says that bliss, to use a Joseph Campbell word , is at the intersection of meaning, competence and enjoyment.

When we are passionate about what we do and also have high-level ability in that area, coupled with enjoying the actual nuts and bolts of the process, we have discovered what we are wired to do; in short, we have found our calling.

The nurses on the intensive care ward all have meaning and should be competent - but, if they discover little enjoyment, then bliss will not be discovered. Unfortunately, many spend decades with employment in which they are not necessarily competent, that provides little meaning and is devoid of enjoyment.

Yet life is not just about doing but about working out who we are and what we are gifted to do. Hard work becomes the natural corollary of this discovery. Laziness then is rarely idleness; simply the result of an uninspired life which simply does not understand its purpose or see clearly its destiny.

INVESTMENT

CLICHÉS LIKE

THE PLAGUE.”

CHAPTER 10

PARTYING WITH PATIENCE

"DISHONEST MONEY DWINDLES AWAY, BUT HE WHO GATHERS MONEY LITTLE BY LITTLE MAKES IT GROW."[32]

The problem with climbing a ladder is that each rung looks the same. The journey of a thousand miles must be covered one mile at a time. The trouble with process... is that it takes so long. Why can't two-year-olds get to five in a few weeks? Why can't teenagers fast track to twenty-one. Whatever we do involves process - writing a book, having a child, building a house, finishing an apprenticeship.

When it comes to building wealth, the willingness to have a long-term mentality and go for it day after day, year after year cannot be underestimated. In our instant society, such thinking is counter-cultural. We are a little bit like the White Rabbit in Alice in Wonderland, "... I'm late, I'm late for a very important date. No time to say hello; goodbye, I'm late... I'm overdue, I'm in a rabbit stew." I wrote in a previous book, Wisdom - The Forgotten Factor of Success, that "we are continually pressed by the supposed lack of time. We talk of being in a rat race, on a treadmill and living during rush hour. We have fast food, instant potatoes and overnight delivery. One comic remarked how a friend of his put instant coffee into a microwave and had a time reversal! Yet, the more time we save, the less we seem to have. We are harried and hurried. Frantic and frenetic, agitated and irritated. In Tennyson's great poem, Ulysses, he talks of, 'living life to the lees'. For many of us, however, we don't even get time to uncork the bottle!"[33]

Yet in building wealth, time is our ally and thus patience must be our guiding principle. Today, the word patience has unfortunately lost a little of its depth. It tends to be a passive word; that is, patience is seen in not getting

"Never buy stocks that won't go up in a bull market - the smart money is out of it."

"Never sell stocks that won't go down in a bear market - the smart money is holding it."

mad in the traffic jam or upset in the automatic teller queue. The word, as it is used in ancient times, however, is positive and proactive. Patience is about sticking at something and not giving in. Something akin to perseverance over the long haul. It has a Churchillian edge to it, "Never, never, never give up."

A lot of people develop the right kind of plan and then change it because results are a little slow. This is like the farmer digging up the crop because he hasn't seen anything happen in the first few weeks. Some things just require time. You cannot rush a fine boeuf bourguignon or more importantly a nine-month pregnancy. Frugality - saving and investing - need time to weave their magic. Rushing the process will destroy all the good work.

Patience then is not about sitting and watching but actively participating in the process. It is the little bit of forward movement each day that makes the difference. Or as my Greek teacher used to say, "It's the daily dose that does it." Physical fitness operates on the same principle; for example my grandmother walks five miles a day and now, after two years ... we haven't got the foggiest idea where she is!

The other benefit of a process mentality is that when there are setbacks or problems they are viewed from a long-range perspective. Thus we will be disappointed but not devastated, knocked down but not knocked out. This kind of patience I can handle because I am making small incremental changes. I am not sitting idly by - my fate in the hands of the croupier. Wealth is not based on Karma or the cards but a confident assurance that the results of right actions over time will yield fruit.

THE PARTY POOPERS

1. Distraction

Glenn Close and Michael Douglas starred in a film called Fatal Attraction yet distraction can be just as fatal. Moving from job to job, church to church, investment strategy to investment strategy can sometimes be wise, but most of the time, such decisions are fuelled by boredom and impatience.

Henry Ford was halfway through constructing his first car when he saw a better way of doing it. His father, however, had always taught him to finish what he started, so finish he did. Later in life he remarked that probably, if he hadn't finished that first one, he would never have finished any.

I have only met a few people of genius in my life but, growing up in New Zealand, there was a guy down the road who could dream the unique and then build it. His material was iron, steel and timber and with it he did wonders. I am sure he could have been a very wealthy man but the moment the challenge of nutting it out was over he moved on to the next project, leaving half-made revolutionary engines, flying machines or farming appliances behind him.

We need to stick with something over time if we intend to enjoy the fruit of our labour. Distraction works against this and can quickly destroy the good plan, good business or, for that matter, the good marriage.

2. The Joneses

The mythical family next door represents colleagues and friends who may in reality or perception be further down wealth's road than us. "Everyone else is...", somehow justifies breaking the plan and cutting the corners. After all we deserve it, as much as or more than them. Human frailty being what it is, we are all prone to such allure, so let us be strong, resist the peer pressure, keep driving the beat-up Kombi and sitting on the older, yet well-loved sofa... our time will come. We are not what we own. Clothes don't make the man - they make the designer rich. Don't let Nike make your statement, make it for yourself.

3. Party Now

"Eat, drink and be merry for tomorrow we die." This is truly stated in the Bible but it is not a statement of truth. As we have already discussed, life is not just a party. Indeed, an eternal dance would soon lose its energy, the participants meandering around the dance floor in a meaningless malaise. No, life is about responsible work and fun. We need both. Judaism upheld a rigorous calendar that was interspersed with days of feasting and rest. In fact, every seventh day was a time-out, the Sabbath. A time for study, prayer and reflection but also celebration.

So, on the journey of wealth it is important to plan many breaks, small rewards, and great parties. To squander all for the good time is to discover that the good time is more than just the party. The goal is not the game, the eating not the meal and the sexual act not the only fun in having a child. Joy is discovered throughout the whole process, whether we are playing a game, cooking a meal or having a child. Certainly this is the case in the subject we are discussing - building wealth over a lifetime.

The power of patience must be employed if we are to continue our journey on the road of wealth...

EPILOGUE

"SO WHAT YOU GONNA DO?"

The purpose of this volume is not just to impart information but also to generate action, to educate and motivate, to provoke thinking and doing. The journey towards wealth, however, does not reside on the learning side. It is the result of application. In order to act correctly and appropriately one must have information, but information is merely step one in a two-step process. Therefore, the question is (to borrow a line from the vultures in Walt Disney's Jungle Book), "what you gonna do?"

Wealth, as we have said from the beginning, is not so much a destination as it is a direction. It is not a snap shot; it is a video. It is not a magic figure but the financial formulation of a life. When we begin to act, we begin to move and when we are moving, we are already becoming wealthy. Already we are becoming part of the answer and not just part of the problem. We are becoming those who can lend a hand and not just one of those who require a handout.

In short, we are becoming wise. For the stupid are the ones who know it all, but the wise are those who slowly but surely begin to act and by so doing, inch their way forward in the direction of their dreams.

"THERE ARE THREE WAYS TO LOSE MONEY: A WOMAN IS THE MOST PLEASURABLE; GAMBLING IS THE FASTEST; AND FARMING IS THE SUREST."

ENDNOTES

1 Lacey, Robert & Danny Danziger, The Year 1000, Little Brown & Co., 1999.

2 Eco, Umberto, Serendipities - Language and Lunacy, Phoenix Publications, London, 1999, pg. 8.

3 Zephyr: The Zephyr's natural habitat was the New Zealand country lane. Made by Ford between 1951 and 1962, they continue to be sadly missed. Check them out at www.motorbase.com/vehicle/vid/1270.html.

4 Stanley, Thomas & William Danko, The Millionaire Next Door, Harper Collins Publishers, Australia, 1988, pg.13.

5 Baker, Philip, Secrets of Super Achievers, Webb & Partners, Perth, Western Australia, pgs. 88, 89, 90 & 92.

6 Genesis 12:2.

7 Book of Proverbs 24:3 & 4.

8 Book of Proverbs 13:11, "He who gathers money little by little makes it grow." .

9 Stanley, Thomas & William Danko, The Millionaire Next Door, Harper Collins Publishers, Australia, 1988, pg 71ff.

10 Book of Proverbs 12:11.

11 Book of Proverbs 21:20.

12 Tobias, Andrew, My Vast Fortune, Harcourt, Brace and Co., 1988, pg. 161.

13 Stanley, Thomas & William Danko, The Millionaire Next Door, Harper Collins Publishers, Australia, 1988, pg. 71ff.

14 Hybels, Bill, Financial Freedom Series, Seeds Tape Resources, Willow Creek, Chicago.

15 Book of Proverbs 27:23 & 24.

16 Book of Proverbs 22:7.

17 Mundis, Jerrold, *How to Get Out of Debt, Stay Out of Debt and Live Prosperously*, Bantam Books, New York, 1988.

18 Whittaker, Noel, *Golden Rules of Wealth*, Simon and Schuster, Australia, 1996, pg. 24.

19 Book of Proverbs 5:8 & 10.

20 Book of Proverbs 6:26.

21 Book of Proverbs 14:15

22 Book of Proverbs 24:27 Living Bible, Tyndale House Publishers, Wheaton, IL, 1971.

23 New Shorter Oxford English Dictionary, Clarindon Press, Oxford, 1993.

24 Hawes, Martin, *Eight Secrets of Investment Success*, Penguin Books, Auckland, 1998, pg. 16.

25 Kiyosaki, Robert, *If You Want to be Rich and Happy Don't go to School*, Aslan Publishing, Lower Lake, California, 1992, pg. 195.

26 Book of Proverbs 11:24, The Message Translation, Navpress, Colorado Springs, CO, 1993.

27 Book of Mark 4:18 & 19.

28 Book of Luke 6:38.

29 Book of Proverbs 16:18, King James Version.

30 Book of Proverbs 6:6-8.

31 Clark, John, *The Money or Your Life*, Tandem Press (NZ) 1997, Ch.8.

32 Book of Proverbs 13:11.

33 Baker, P., *Wisdom - The Forgotten Factor of Success*, Webb & Partners, 1999, pg. 173.

ABOUT THE AUTHOR

Phil Baker is one of Australia's leading speakers, who has the ability to combine solid content with a practical, humorous and dynamic delivery.

He is also the author of several other books, including:

- The Best Seller - Secrets of Super Achievers

- The Best Seller - Attitudes of Amazing Achievers

- Wisdom - The Forgotten Factor of Success

Having been born in England, raised in new Zealand, he now resides in Perth, Western Australia where he pastors a contemporary church, Riverview Church, [www.riverviewchurch.com.au], in Burswood, which attracts over 2400 people at its key weekend services.

Phil is married to Heather and they have three girls, Jazmin, Temily and Isabel.

NOTES

NOTES